MAPLE TREE PRESS

ONLY IN CANADA!

WRITTEN BY

VIVIEN BOWERS

ILLUSTRATED BY
DIANNE EASTMAN

Canadian
Moose

Owl Books are published by Maple Tree Press Inc.
51 Front Street East, Suite 200, Toronto, Ontario M5E 1B3

The Owl colophon is a trademark of Owl Children's Trust Inc.
Maple Tree Press Inc. is a licensed user of trademarks of
Owl Children's Trust Inc.

Canada
Goose

Distributed in the United States by
Firefly Books (U.S.) Inc. 230 Fifth Avenue,
Suite 1607, New York, NY 10001

We acknowledge the financial support of the Canada
Council for the Arts, the Ontario Arts Council, and the
Government of Canada through the Book Publishing Industry
Development Program (BPIDP) for our publishing activities.

Cataloguing in Publication Data
Bowers, Vivien, 1951–
    Only in Canada! : from the colossal to the kooky
(A Wow Canada! book)
Includes index.
ISBN 1-894379-37-3 (bound)   ISBN 1-894379-38-1 (pbk.)
1. Canada—Juvenile literature.
2. Canada—Miscellanea—Juvenile literature.
I. Eastman, Dianne.   II. Title.   III. Series: Wow Canada! book.

FC58.B684   2002   j971   C2002-900411-X
F1008.2.B68 2002

Design & art direction: Dianne Eastman
Illustrations: Dianne Eastman
Photo credits: See page 94

Printed in Hong Kong

A   B   C   D   E   F

Contents

For goodness sake, don't do that to me, Goose! You just about gave
me a heart attack.
    I figure you need shaking up, Moose. You need excitement in your life.
    My life is plenty exciting, thanks. I don't need geese landing on my head.
        Look at you—stuck here in boring old Canada.
    Canada is not boring!
        I fly down south every winter, and when I come back in the spring,
            you still have your big nose in a Canadian bog. You're bogged down!
    Well, for your information, bogs are fascinating places. And they're
        just one reason why Canada is definitely not boring.
            You're sure?
            Absolutely! Canada is full of fascinating facts, peculiar places,
                hilarious history, and perplexing people. It's mystifying,
                    mind-boggling, totally unbelievable, wacky, weird, and wonderful
                        stuff. Want me to show you?
                        You bet! Let's moose-y along right now. I mean, mosey along.
                            I mean ... Let's go!
                            Follow me.

You're sure this isn't going to be some wild moose chase?

No more bad jokes, okay?

I make no promises.

Chapter 1

Amazing Facts about How Canada Was Bashed, Pummelled, Scrunched, and Scraped into the Shape It's in Today

Want to find out how Canada got to be so bashed, pummelled, and scraped? Prepare to fast-forward through millions of years of geologic time. The earth will shudder, asteroids will crash, and (watch out!) rocks will tumble. Geography is exciting stuff!

Catastrophic collisions of the earth's plates

Geography gone amok

Earthquakes that will knock your socks off

Massive ice sheets oozing onward

Huge rocks crashing to earth

Erosion is awfully S-L-O-W! Where's all this action you promised?

You want action? Right this way!

Look at Canada, Goose—a huge chunk of rock with ocean on three sides.

Have you ever wondered why Canada is the shape it is?

Nope.

Well, you should wonder more, Goose. It's a good habit to get into.

Okay. I wonder why Canada is the shape it is.

I'll give you the short answer, even though the story actually took place over billions of years. Take those mountains down there as an example. They are the result of a long-ago collision between two of the huge plates that make up the earth's crust.

Some collison! It looks like the landscape was totalled.

And see the white patches below? Those are glaciers—sheets of ice. At times in the past, most of Canada was covered in ice like that, only thicker. Those ice sheets did some heavy-duty landscaping of the country.

You mean landscraping!

Very good, Goose! And ever since the ice ages, Canada's landscape has continued to be worn down and shaped by erosion.

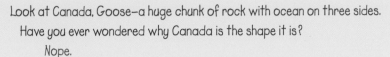

Proceed
with Caution:
Careering
Continents
Ahead

Careering Continents

Somebody file an accident report!

The plates that make up the earth's crust are slowly drifting about and crashing into each other like bumper cars. It's true! Canada, which rides on the North American plate, bears the scars and dents of massive collisions that have occurred over the past few billion years.

And guess what? Those plates are still moving. Don't look now, but we're on another collision course!

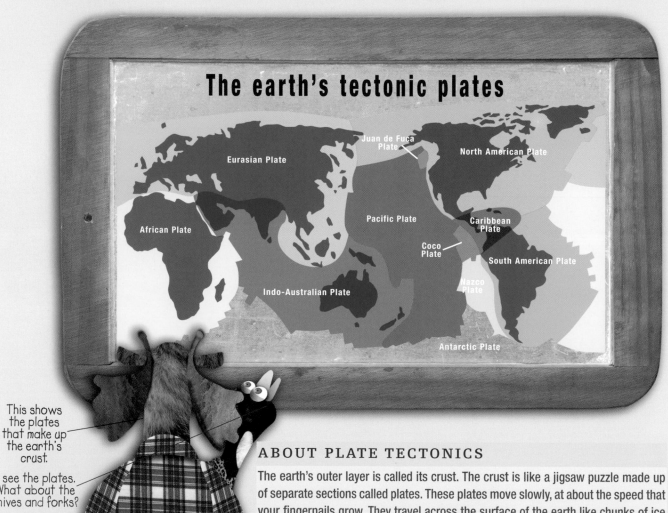

The earth's tectonic plates

Eurasian Plate

Juan de Fuca Plate

North American Plate

African Plate

Pacific Plate

Caribbean Plate

Coco Plate

South American Plate

Indo-Australian Plate

Nazco Plate

Antarctic Plate

This shows the plates that make up the earth's crust.

I see the plates. What about the knives and forks?

ABOUT PLATE TECTONICS

The earth's outer layer is called its crust. The crust is like a jigsaw puzzle made up of separate sections called plates. These plates move slowly, at about the speed that your fingernails grow. They travel across the surface of the earth like chunks of ice floating on a lake. For hundreds of millions of years, they've been colliding and then drifting apart again. The continent of North America, which of course includes Canada, is being carried along on the North American plate.

When plates collide, one can be shoved under the other, deep into the earth, where it melts. When plates drift apart or develop cracks (called faults), hot magma (liquefied rock) from inside the earth rises up through the gap, cools, and then hardens to form new crust.

CANADA: SMASHED TOGETHER FROM COAST TO COAST

Imagine taking an old chunk of modelling clay and then jamming new clay onto each side. When you pull the new clay off again, some of it might remain stuck to the older clay. The continent of North America was formed like that. The original part of the continent (which includes the Canadian Shield) is made of rock that's billions of years old. It was later rammed from both sides by colliding plates, and each collision added some new rock to what was there in the beginning. (And you thought hockey was a rough game!)

Four hundred million years ago, what is now eastern North America received a hit from Europe and Africa. That collision squished up the Appalachian Mountains. When Europe and Africa split off again, some pieces got left behind. Today there is still rock from Europe and Africa stuck to Newfoundland and Nova Scotia.

The newest rock in North America is found on the West Coast. It's actually different from the rock that makes up the rest of Canada, because it was stuck on to the continent later. That collision also bulldozed, scrunched, and folded the landscape into some very scenic mountains in British Columbia and the Yukon.

EXCEEDINGLY WEIRD

High in the Rocky Mountains, thousands of metres above sea level, there are reefs that originally formed under the ocean 365 million years ago! How did these ancient reefs end up on top of a mountain? These things happen when plate collisions make a total mess of the landscape.

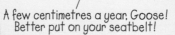

9

Extreme Geography

You've heard of extreme sports, right? How about extreme geography? A lot of weird stuff has happened to Canada's landscape over the past billion years or so. It's enough to make you wonder what will happen next.

LOOK UP! LOOK DOWN!

Head for the Great Lakes and set your time machine back more than a billion years. Imagine a towering mountain range, higher than any mountains on earth today. Evidence found in the rocks proves that these mountains once stretched from Labrador through the Great Lakes region and down to Mexico. They were the result of an ancient collision between continental plates. Ouch!

If you travel forward 100 million years from there, you might be able to see the world's deepest canyon. This gigantic chasm almost cut the North American continent in two. They just don't make geography like that any more.

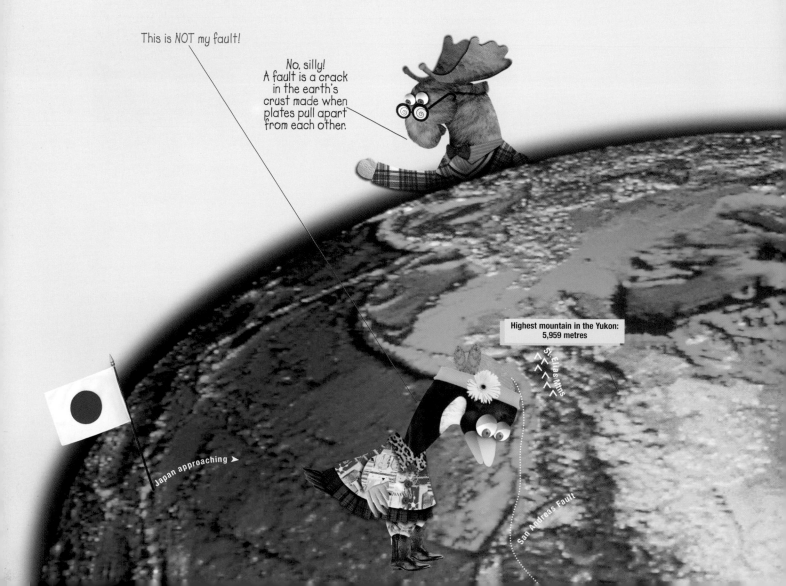

This is NOT my fault!

No, silly! A fault is a crack in the earth's crust made when plates pull apart from each other.

Highest mountain in the Yukon: 5,959 metres

St. Elias Mtns

Japan approaching ▶

San Andreas Fault

COLLISION COURSE

Uh, oh. The North American continent is on a collision course with Asia! The Atlantic Ocean is getting wider (because the plates under the ocean are moving away from each other), and the Pacific Ocean is getting narrower (because underwater plates are sliding under each other). The result is that North America is inching towards Asia. In a few hundred million years, people on Vancouver Island may look out their windows and be able to wave to their neighbours—in Japan!

CANADA SEPARATING?

On a map, look at the shape of New Brunswick and Nova Scotia. See how the Bay of Fundy seems to split them apart? That's not far from the truth. Remember that long-ago collision, when the Europe and Africa plate smashed into the North American plate and then pulled away again? Well, the island we now call Nova Scotia was almost ripped away from the rest of the North American plate. The earth's crust partially separated, forming the gap that became the Bay of Fundy.

VISIT CANADA'S TROPICS

About 400 million years ago, Canadians wouldn't have needed to fly south for a tropical holiday—Canada *was* farther south. The North American plate was drifting near the equator at the time. If we'd been around then, maybe we could have gone snorkelling in a tropical sea.

But eventually, the North American plate drifted north, bringing Canada with it. Now all we have to remind us of those good old days in the hot sun are 400-million-year-old coral fossils.

DON'T LOOK DOWN

The tall peaks of the St. Elias Mountains in northern B.C. and the Yukon include Mount Logan, the highest mountain in Canada (at 5,959 metres). As if they weren't high enough already, these mountains are rising even more. This is because the Pacific plate is ramming in underneath the edge of the North American plate, jacking up the mountains. They are rising *really* fast, according to geologists. Maybe as much as four millimetres a year.

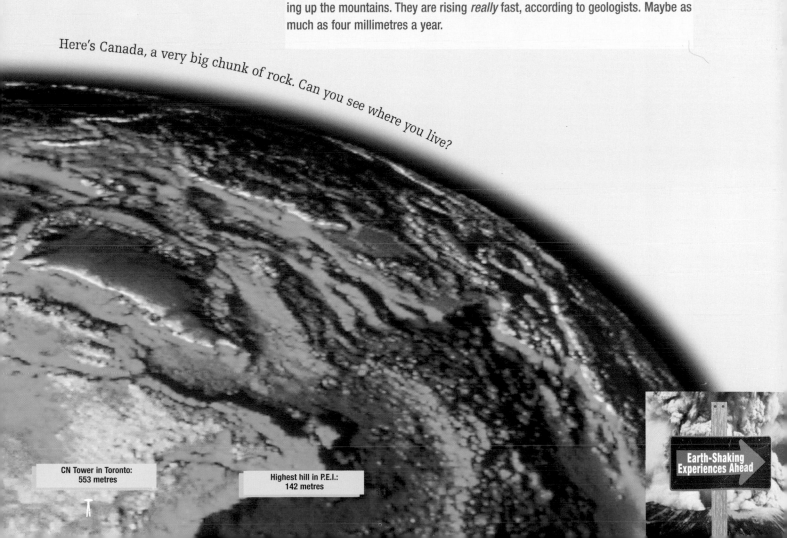

Here's Canada, a very big chunk of rock. Can you see where you live?

CN Tower in Toronto: 553 metres

Highest hill in P.E.I.: 142 metres

Earth-Shaking Experiences Ahead

On Shaky Ground

The most earth-shaking place in Canada is near the Pacific Coast, where one plate is jammed against another. When these two plates grind against each other, the ground shakes, shudders, and trembles. For goodness quake, hold on tight! Where there are earthquakes, you may find tsunamis and volcanoes too!

WHAT'S MAGNITUDE?

The magnitude of an earthquake is a measurement of how much energy the earthquake releases. There is a scale, called the Richter scale, which begins at 0 and goes to 10. An earthquake with a magnitude of less than 5 is very unlikely to cause any damage. But each successive number on the scale represents a quake that is thirty-two times more powerful than one at the previous number. In other words, a magnitude 6 earthquake is thirty-two times stronger than a magnitude 5 quake. A magnitude 7 quake is about a thousand times stronger than a magnitude 5 quake. A magnitude 8 quake is ... definitely TOO big!

THE BIG ONE

It happened about 300 years ago. On the night of January 26, 1700, one of the world's greatest earthquakes occurred off the West Coast of the United States. Because the quake had an estimated magnitude of 9, it is certain that the Native people living on the Pacific coast of Canada at the time would have felt the shaking.

How can scientists know the date of the earthquake when written records were not yet being kept in this part of the world? It generated a tsunami (a giant wave) that swept across the Pacific Ocean to Japan, and the damage caused by the tsunami was well recorded there. Scientists used this written information to calculate the time, size, and location of the original earthquake.

COMING SOON ... THE NEXT BIG ONE?

In British Columbia, people living near the coast have been told to prepare for another big earthquake. Just west of Vancouver Island, the Juan de Fuca plate, which has been sliding under the North American plate, has become stuck—and the pressure is building. Eventually, the two plates will break loose again, causing a tremendous earthquake.

Scientists predict that the shaking from this quake could last several minutes. When it stops, some places along the coast will be one to two metres lower than they were before. They will also have shifted about ten metres out to sea.

It could happen hundreds of years from now ... or perhaps next week.

MILKSHAKES?

Canada's biggest quake ever (magnitude 8.1) occurred along the western coast of the Queen Charlotte Islands, in British Columbia, on August 22, 1949. The shaking apparently knocked cows off their feet.

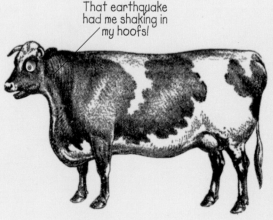

VOLCANOES—THAR SHE BLOWS!

Volcanoes often occur at the edges of tectonic plates. As the edge of a plate descends deep into the earth, it melts. Molten rock then rises up and bursts through the earth's crust to form volcanoes.

Even in Canada? You bet. Volcanic action is a little slow at the moment, but about 2,350 years ago, there was a stupendous volcanic eruption about 160 kilometres north of Vancouver. Mount Meager exploded with the power of ten hydrogen bombs, blasting ash and hot rock into the air.

Canadian volcanoes that have been active during the past few hundred years can be found in British Columbia and the Yukon. Check out Nisga'a Memorial Lava Bed Provincial Park and Mount Edziza Provincial Park.

Mount Edziza

Surf's up!

TSUNAMI STORY

When an underwater earthquake makes the ground move, the sea above it also moves up or down. This creates a series of waves called a tsunami. If you were on a ship out in the deep ocean, you wouldn't even feel a tsunami because the waves would be small and far apart (as much as 200 kilometres apart). When the tsunami reaches shallow water, however, the waves become much higher and can strike the shore with devastating force.

WAVE HELLO!

Tsunamis don't happen often, but they can be impressive! On November 18, 1929, the most destructive earthquake ever to hit Canada's East Coast occurred. Two hundred and fifty kilometres south of Newfoundland, an earthquake under the ocean floor caused an underwater landslide that ripped up telegraph cables that had been laid down on the seabed. It also created a tsunami that surged at a speed of 140 kilometres an hour towards Newfoundland's south coast. Like a three-metre-high battering ram, the tsunami tossed boats onto the shore and swept away waterfront houses. Twenty-nine people died.

It was the middle of the night on March 27, 1964, when the biggest North American earthquake in a century occurred off the coast of Alaska. The quake created a huge tsunami that crashed into the Alaskan coast, killing one hundred people, and then swept down British Columbia at speeds of up to 720 kilometres an hour. In Port Alberni, which lies at the head of a long inlet on the west coast of Vancouver Island, the tsunami swept through the town, uprooting homes, snapping hydro poles, and carrying away cars. Some people opened their front and back doors and let the water pass through their houses. Others had to flee in darkness. Miraculously, nobody was killed.

Cold Front Approaching

Ice Time

Prepare for thrills and chills! We're heading back to the ice ages—periods during the past few million years when up to 97 per cent of Canada was covered by thick sheets of ice. We've got more glacier-gouged land than any other country. Imagine—the ice was three kilometres thick in some places!

Glaciers can really do damage to the landscape. As they slowly advance and retreat, they scrape, scour, and smooth out the mountains. They dump piles of sand and gravel. They sometimes even block rivers and form huge lakes. When the ice melts and the glaciers have retreated, what's left? The landscape of Canada as it is today!

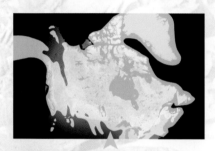

You can see how much of Canada was covered by glaciers during the last ice age. Today glaciers are found only on high mountains or in the Far North.

ON THE REBOUND

When a heavy person steps off a floating dock—boing!—it rises. Something similar happened after the ice ages. The heavy ice sheets weighting down the land retreated and—boing!—the land in eastern Canada has been rising ever since. (Scientists don't say "boing"; they call it rebounding.) Here are some remarkable rebounding facts:

- The land around Hudson Bay is rebounding at the rate of about 0.6 centimetres each year. The bay is getting shallower, and one day (in about a million gazillion years) it could be high and dry!

- When ice weighted down the land on the north shore of the Great Lakes, they used to tilt to that side. Now that the ice has retreated, the lakes are gradually tilting more towards the south.

- When the last ice sheets melted 14,000 years ago, the sea level rose. The rising water partly flooded Prince Edward Island, leaving only the highest land above water, in the form of three smaller islands. Then the land rebounded, rising up out of the sea and turning P.E.I. back into the one island we know today.

The ice ages? Br r r r r! I'm turning into frozen poultry!

You're the one with the goose-down jacket.

14

ICE-FREE ZONE

Hold on—not all of Canada was covered with ice! On the Queen Charlotte Islands, there are plants and animals that aren't found anywhere else in Canada. That's because the islands were ice-free.

Some high mountain peaks in the Yukon and the Northwest Territories also poked up above the ice, as did the tops of the Cypress Hills, in Alberta and southern Saskatchewan. Those areas were cold enough for glaciers, but they were too dry (that is, they didn't have enough snow) for ice to form.

NO FERRY LINEUPS

It's a seven-hour ferry-boat ride from the British Columbia mainland to the Queen Charlotte Islands today. Thirteen thousand years ago, you could have walked there across land. With so much of the world's water frozen during the ice ages, sea levels were much lower.

MESSY GLACIERS

Did you know glaciers were messy? They carried tons of rock and dirt as they flowed across the landscape. When they melted, they dumped their loads and left them behind. (If you tried that at home, your parents would make you clean up after yourself!) Dumped rocks (called erratics) and walls of dirt and rock (called moraines) are signs that a glacier once scraped through the neighbourhood.

Queen Charlotte Islands

Thousand Islands

Prairie Erratic

Who left this boulder in the middle of the prairies?

ROCK BOTTOM

The rocky landscape we call the Canadian Shield covers much of Canada. The Shield is like a huge circular saucer, with Hudson Bay as its centre. Over millions of years, glaciers scraped the top layer of ground down to the old, old rock below. The oldest rock in the world (about 4 billion years old) is found not far from the city of Yellowknife, in the Northwest Territories.

Here's a Canadian sword to go with the Canadian Shield.

LEFTOVER ISLANDS

There used to be a mountain range as tall as the Rockies in the St. Lawrence River, then the glaciers scraped the mountains down to size. Now all that's left of them are the Thousand Islands!

Goose, you're kidding me, right?

UNDERWATER FOREST

In Georgian Bay, on Lake Superior, scuba divers can explore an underwater forest that's 7,600 years old. The water level was lower just after the ice sheets retreated from this area. At that time, the forest grew above water, along the base of a cliff. As the water level rose, the forest drowned. But the cold water has helped preserve it.

Boulders like this made dandy rubbing stones for bison.

It takes something big to make a sizeable dent in the Canadian landscape—such as an asteroid! When asteroids from space slam into earth, the shock waves from the impact blast out huge craters. Fortunately, asteroids don't turn up very often. Still, Canada does have twenty-six big impact craters to show where asteroids have landed in the past. That's more than any other country. There's no telling when additional extraterrestrial objects might drop in.

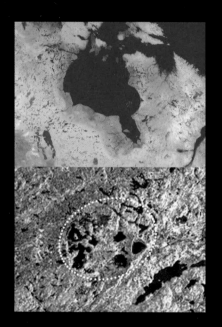

THE MYSTERIOUS MONSTER METEOR OF HUDSON BAY

Take a look at a map of Hudson Bay. Notice the rounded bite that seems to have been munched from the east shoreline (on the right)? It's shaped like one side of a perfect circle that's centred around the Belcher Islands. Scientists have looked at this shape and wondered if it could be the edge of a stupendous meteor-impact crater.

SUDBURY CRATER

At 250 kilometres across, this is Canada's biggest crater. It was likely caused by the impact of a monstrous asteroid 1.85 billion years ago. It was a blast!

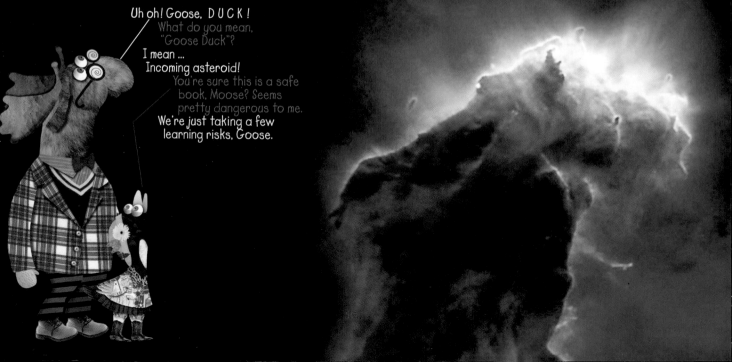

Made quite an impact, eh?

CRATÈRE DE NOUVEAU QUEBEC

This asteroid hit the northern tip of Quebec in the Ungava region, east of Hudson Bay, quite recently—a mere 1.4 million years ago. Scientists think the asteroid was 200 metres across. It made a hole in the ground that's three kilometres wide and 264 metres deep. Today it looks like a perfectly round lake with crystal clear water, but there are no streams running in or out of it. That would seem mighty odd—unless you knew how the lake was created!

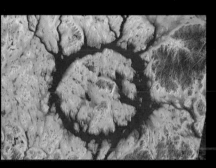

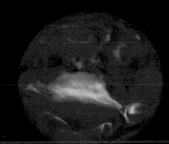

MANICOUGAN RESERVOIR

Asteroid, disasteroid! Some 214 million years ago, a huge asteroid believed to have been five kilometres wide slammed into Quebec. (Well, actually, this was somewhat before it was called Quebec.) The impact was 150,000 times as powerful as that of the atomic bomb that was dropped on Hiroshima. You can see the round impact crater, which measures one hundred kilometres across, in this satellite photo. (It's full of water because the crater is now the reservoir of a nearby dam.)

WELCOME TO MARS

On a frigid, rocky, uninhabited island in Canada's High Arctic, scientists have found Mars—or as close as they are likely to get to it without leaving earth. A giant meteorite crashed on Devon Island 23 million years ago. The impact blasted shards of rocks thousands of metres into the sky. Today the landscape is cold, dry, and rocky—quite like the planet Mars! Scientists from NASA are using this site to do experiments that they hope will help them when astronauts really do visit Mars.

TERRESTRIAL CRASH LANDING

Not all big things that go bump in the night come from space. Rock slides can significantly shape the landscape too.

The most disastrous rock slide in Canadian history was the Frank slide. It happened in the Rocky Mountains of south-eastern Alberta at 4:10 a.m. on April 29, 1903. A huge chunk of Turtle Mountain let loose and crashed down the slope towards the sleeping town of Frank. Part of the town disappeared under rock, and seventy people died. Rocks covered three square kilometres of the valley bottom, up to a depth of fifty metres.

On the other side of the country, in parts of eastern Ontario and western Quebec, the topsoil covers a thick clay that can turn into a mucky, slippery mass. There have been thousands of landslides in this area. On May 4, 1971, a landslide at St-Jean-Vianney, Quebec, destroyed thirty-six homes and killed thirty-one people in just five minutes. In June 1993, a man driving along the banks of the South Nation River, east of Ottawa, suddenly found himself hanging upside down in his truck at the bottom of a landslide, with two broken arms and other injuries. The clay had turned to liquid. Flowing like wet cement, it had carried the ground, trees, and road down into the river.

Chapter 2

Naturally and Wildly Canadian

Pack your binoculars and mammoth repellent! We're off on safari to discover the weird, intriguing, obnoxious, badly behaved, and utterly improbable plants and animals that exist in Canada. It's wild out there!

Animals that grin and bear it through Arctic winters

Creatures that really go far

Bizarre critters that used to exist

Odd, obnoxious, or outlandish animals

Astounding but true facts about Canadian animals

Particularly peculiar plants

Weird partnerships between animals and plants

So what's up ahead?

Whatever it is, I bet it will be wild!

Say, Goose. I'll bet you didn't know that Canada has more
than a million square kilometres of muskeg.
Wow, that's amazing! Er ... what's muskeg?
Bog. Muskeg is a special Canadian word for bog. It's from the Cree language.
As in squishy, squooshy, goopy, gucky, slimy, swampy bog?
We've got more of it than any other country.
Is that good?
Great! Especially for moose. Actually, lots of plants and animals like bogs.
Such as frogs! Get it? A frog in the bog.
There are also lots of insects in bogs.
"Insects" doesn't rhyme.
Frogs like them, though. Plants eat insects too.
Very funny! They do not.
Oh yes, they do. Carnivorous plants in bogs actually eat
insects!
Yikes! That's very weird.
Let's go and find some other exceedingly weird
animals and plants that lurk in Canada's bogs,
rainforests, grasslands, tundra—all over
this huge country! Big and small, from
mammoths to nose bots!
Nose bots?
You'll see!

NORTH
To the Arctic!

Antifreeze and Other Ways to Survive a Canadian Arctic Winter

Brrrrrrrrrrrrrrrr! Canada specializes in toe-tingling, finger-freezing winters, especially in its Far North. From long underwear to leg warmers, Arctic animals have come up with ingenious ways to survive the cold.

POLAR PROS

Polar bears have so much fat and warm fur that they actually overheat if they get too energetic. Their hairs are hollow and trap air for added insulation (the same way that a layer of air trapped in a down jacket becomes warmed by your body heat and acts as a barrier against the cold).

Polar bears also have amazing paws. They have fur on the bottom of their paws so they don't slip on the ice and look silly. And they have webbed toes that act as snowshoes when they walk and flippers when they swim. Swimming in winter? Not as crazy as it sounds. At least the water temperature is warmer than the air!

COLD FEET

You wouldn't walk around barefoot on the ice in winter—and caribou don't either. In summer, the caribou's foot pads touch the ground. But in winter, the caribou's hoofs grow longer, lifting the foot pads until they're off the ground. Voila—high-heeled snow boots!

Here's another clever trick that caribou, and some birds, have. When their feet are stuck in cold snow, they don't waste energy heating their legs. They pump warm blood around the main parts of their bodies to keep their temperature at about 40°C, but they let their legs cool to 10°C.

BRRRRRRR BIRRRRRRRDS

A one-legged bird? No, that Arctic bird is simply standing motionless on one leg, with the other bent up against its belly and its beak tucked under its wing. It is trying to keep its outer parts from freezing. Keeping still helps the bird conserve energy, and it uses its own body heat to keep its leg and beak warm. You do the same thing when you tuck your hands into your pockets. But how long can you stand on one leg?

Frozen for the season. Please call again next spring.
Signed, Arctic Woolly Bear Caterpillar

EXCEEDINGLY WEIRD

The Arctic woolly bear caterpillar freezes solid each winter. In spring, this large orange fuzzy-wuzzy thaws out to continue its life cycle. It may take fourteen short Arctic summers before this caterpillar is finally ready to make a cocoon and change into an adult moth. Then it has to hurry to find a mate and lay its eggs because it can't survive the winter deep-freeze as a moth.

GREAT LONG UNDERWEAR

Muskoxen are the only animals that don't seek shelter during incredibly brutal Arctic blizzards. Of course, muskoxen dress for the weather, just like your parents tell you to do. Their "long underwear" is made of a wool that's much warmer than sheep's wool. Over top, there's a shaggy "skirt" made of long guard hairs. Not chic, but definitely warm.

Ummmm. I forgot to check my antifreeze this winter.

Moose, did you know some insects make their own "antifreeze" to prevent the liquid in their cells from freezing?

Astounding Canadian Travellers

Some animals have figured out a better way to cope with Canada's winter—they head south! Other animals migrate for different reasons. Check out these wild travel adventures.

FLUTTER POWER

Each autumn, millions of monarch butterflies migrate south to their wintering grounds. They fly up to 4,000 kilometres from the Great Lakes to a few mountain forests in southern Mexico, often choosing the same trees that were wintered in the year before by their relatives. When spring arrives, the longer days prompt the butterflies to head north again.

Here's something else that's really amazing. The monarch butterfly that rides the winds from Canada down to Mexico in the autumn is not the same one that returns in the spring. Monarchs don't live that long. Three to five generations are born and die during the trip home. It's like a relay race, where one monarch flies partway north before producing the next generation and so on. Yet somehow the returning butterflies find their way to the exact starting point on the Great Lakes, even though they have never been there before.

This is a very moving story.

COMING THROUGH!

It's a mob scene! Caribou migrate across the Canadian North in huge herds. They travel from the tundra, where they give birth to their calves, to wintering grounds that may be as much as a thousand kilometres away. From a plane over the tundra, you can see paths that have been pounded into the land from years of caribou use.

The George River caribou herd is the record-breaker. Some 800,000 animals trek 9,000 kilometres around northern Quebec—the longest land migration in North America. But come spring, no matter where they are, they make a beeline to their calving grounds on the Ungava Peninsula, near Hudson Bay.

22

You can't stop yet— we're not at the spawning grounds.

I know, but some days it's such an uphill battle.

Got any cheap flights to Mexico?

What do you do in Antarctica?

I tern around.

BY LEAPS AND BOUNDS

Salmon migrations are just plain astounding. Adult fish lay their eggs in freshwater streams. Once hatched, the new salmon swim downstream to the ocean, where they spend the next several years. When they are themselves ready to spawn, they find their way back to the very same rivers where they were born. They battle their way upstream, leaping over rapids and obstacles, and finally end where they started. The trip up the river can be more than a thousand kilometres. After laying and fertilizing eggs on the gravel at the spawning grounds, the worn-out fish usually die. (And who can blame them!)

HUMDINGER!

Hummingbirds flap their wings really quickly—about 3,000 wingbeats per minute, or fifty per second. So imagine what an effort it must be when a tiny hummingbird migrating from Canada gets down to the Gulf of Mexico and has to fly across 800 kilometres of water without a rest. That's a non-stop flight of about 5 million wingbeats lasting all day and night. Phew!

MOST FREQUENT FLYER POINTS

The award for long-distance travel goes to a small black, white, and grey seabird, the Arctic tern (also called a sea swallow). Each autumn, it makes an incredible 30,000-kilometre round trip from its breeding grounds in the Arctic to a spot near Antarctica (where the tern can enjoy summer during Canada's winter) and back again in the spring.

Pacific grey whales found off the coast of British Columbia migrate farther than any other mammal— a 16,000-kilometre round trip from Alaska to Mexico.

EXTINCTION
ZONE
AHEAD

Unbelievable Animals That Really Existed in Canada

Enter a twilight zone of improbable-looking creatures that—believe it or not—actually existed in Canada. With strange beasts like these, who needs science fiction?

EXCEEDINGLY WEIRD

Do you believe that camels once lived in B.C.? You should—it's true! Well, they weren't actually wild camels, and they weren't natural to the area. During British Columbia's gold rush in 1862, someone had the brilliant plan to import camels to pack supplies up the Cariboo Wagon Road to the goldfields. It turned out not to be such a brilliant idea. The two-humped camels were used to soft desert sand, so they needed little booties to protect their feet from the rocky road. They bit and kicked at everything, and smelled awful. After four months they were banned from the Cariboo Wagon Road. Some escaped and lived in the wild for a short time before they died.

CREATURES FROM THE BURGESS SHALE

Imagine a creature with five eyes, a nozzle like a vacuum-cleaner hose sticking out from its head, and a crab-like claw at the end of the nozzle. Freaky! Or imagine a tube-bodied creature with a head shaped like a light bulb. Its rear end turns up like a bent straw, it walks on seven pairs of stilt-like legs, and seven tentacles stick up out of its back.

These creatures really did exist in Canada. Scientists have discovered the most remarkable collection of fossils in the world in the Rocky Mountains. The fossils date back to a period 530 million years ago. At that time, the Rocky Mountains didn't exist and the landscape looked very different. The area was an underwater reef that was home to many small (and weird-looking) animals. When they died, the animals were buried in fine silt that later hardened into a rock called shale. The shale now shows the imprint of their bodies. These Burgess Shale fossils tell us that Canada was once home to bizarre creatures unlike anything living today.

ICE AGE MONSTERS

Large, extra large, and mammoth! Fossils dug up in the Yukon prove that these were the sizes of the amazing behemoths that once lived in what is now Canada. These giants roamed the dry, grassy plains of a long-ago land called Beringia. Beringia also included a wide land bridge linking North America to Asia during the ice ages, when sea levels were lower.

Besides enormous, elephant-like woolly mammoths and mastodons, there were beavers the size of black bears with teeth up to fifteen centimetres long (imagine the grin!), giant bears (larger than any existing today) with bulldog-like faces, ground sloths the size of oxen, and predators you might not want to meet, such as a wildcat twice as big as a cougar, with fangs like steak knives and a top speed of sixty kilometres an hour.

Look at that weird animal with the long nose! It's called a moose.

Have you ever seen anything so ludicrous?

Are you talking about me?

DINOSAURS

It's still hard to believe that creatures as huge and fantastic as dinosaurs roamed Canada 70 million years ago. Luckily for us, one of the best collection of dinosaur bones in the world is in southeastern Alberta (at Dinosaur Provincial Park). The area was once a swampy forest along the shore of a warm inland sea.

Paleontologists have found all shapes and sizes of dinosaur skeletons. This makes it easier to picture what the real things must have looked like. Some sported horns or crests on their heads. Some had spikes along their backs. Some were armed like tanks, with bony clubs at the ends of their tails. Many had funny flat snouts like duck bills. One plant-eater had as many as 2,000 teeth in its jaws. (Imagine the dental bills!)

Dinosaur fossils have been found in other parts of Canada too. The biggest *Tyrannosaurus rex* fossil was discovered at Eastend, in southern Saskatchewan. It was about as long as a school bus and as tall as a two-storey house.

Hey, I know another weird creature—the sasquatch!
It's a hairy, ape-like monster that some people believe actually exists.
Entirely unbelievable, I'm afraid. Just like Ogopogo, that swimming monster that supposedly lives in the depths of Okanagan Lake in B.C.
You're right, it's entirely unbelievable.
Just like...a talking moose!
Well, now that you mention it...

Where the Weird Things Are

A Selection of Canada's Most Odd, Obnoxious, or Outlandish Animals

Here's the moment you've been waiting for. Introducing a sampling of Canada's oddest, yuckiest, and strangest animals. Not a cute and cuddly one among them!

Wow! Did you see the size of that fish?

Oh, sure. Another fish story.

Do you ever wonder what's the point?

Nope.

I reuse and recycle roadkill.

STURGEON

Hundred-year-old white sturgeon are truly monstrous, mysterious mega-fish of the deeps! In 1887, a fisherman on B.C.'s Fraser River caught a 630-kilogram specimen (about the weight of eight men) that was 5.5 metres long (as long as a Volkswagen Beetle). Because of its spines and rows of sharp bony bumps, plus its shark-like tail, Canada's largest fish has no predators—apart from humans, of course.

NARWHALS

Kings once paid a fortune for unicorn horns, often inlaid with rubies and other precious stones. A unicorn's horn was said to have magic healing powers. Psssst! Want to know a secret? These "unicorn horns" came not from a white horse, but from a little Arctic whale. (When this was discovered, the price of unicorn horn plummeted.)

Introducing the narwhal! Strange-looking indeed, male narwhals have a long, spiralled, horn-like tooth that extends two to three metres from the gums. Most of the world's narwhals live in the Arctic seas, between Canada and Greenland.

EXCEEDINGLY WEIRD

Nose bots and warble flies are two revolting bugs that make a caribou's life miserable. The nose bot (that's really its name) is a large hairy fly that goes up the caribou's nose and lays its young there. The squirmy maggots then travel up the caribou's nasal passages to the entrance to its throat. Here they eat and grow into a big lump. The caribou keeps coughing and sneezing, until eventually it sneezes out the lump of nose bots! By this time, the larvae are fully grown. They are ready to pupate in the soil and become flies. Scientists suspect that the discomfort caused by nose bots sometimes makes caribou stampede. No wonder!

The warble fly is another disgusting caribou parasite. This fly lays her eggs on caribou hairs. When they hatch, the maggots burrow into and under the caribou's skin and grow there all winter. They even cut little breathing holes for themselves. In the spring, the maggots drop out through the holes to the ground, where they pupate and eventually turn into flies. A single caribou may feed 2,000 uninvited warble fly maggots.

TURKEY VULTURES

Don't invite this one for dinner. A turkey vulture eats rotten, decaying meat. To feed its young, the vulture swallows all the food it can, then vomits it up for its chicks. The smell is so awful it repels predators.

I'm not sure I can stomach that.

THE FEARSOME PREDATOR OF THE SEASHORE

Thought it was a starfish? It's actually not a fish, and its real name is the sea star. Most sea stars have five arms, but the sunflower sea star has twenty-four. This is handy because if one arm gets ripped off, it has plenty of others to use until the missing arm grows back.

Sea stars are the silent, stealthy, voracious predators of Canada's seashores. A big sunflower sea star can be nearly a metre wide (about as far as you can stretch both arms). It seems to glide across the rocks on its 15,000 tiny, muscular tube feet. Each foot is equipped with a suction cup.

Sea stars have appalling table manners when they eat. Instead of putting food into their stomachs, they put their stomachs into their food! The sea star pushes its stomach out of its mouth (the mouth is under the body, in the centre of all those arms), basically turning the stomach inside out. When it wraps this stomach around a clam, one of its favourite foods, it will push in between the two shells to digest the soft body inside. Would you call that eating out?

GREAT BALLS OF SNAKES!

Manitoba has the world's largest population of red-sided garter snakes. When it comes time for them to hibernate for the winter, up to 10,000 snakes pack themselves together into a huge ball to conserve heat in their underground den. In spring, as the sun warms the air, they leave their den. Mating fever turns the snakes into a gigantic, writhing, wriggling tangle!

Moose are excellent blood donors. A moose can lose up to a cupful of blood a day from horseflies.

Some Astounding But True, Little-Known Facts about Canadian Animals

In which we reveal some of the bizarre habits and curious behaviours of several Canadian animals.

That's a counterfeit bill!

PUFFINS wear false bills! Puffins are little birds with brightly coloured, oversized bills. But it's all for show! After the puffins finish courting, the birds ditch the colourful outer plates. Underneath there's a much less impressive real bill—smaller and quite drab.

Another thing you probably didn't know about seabirds like puffins is that they have runny noses. They dribble a salty liquid out through nostrils in their bills. It's their way of getting rid of the excess salt they accumulate after gulping down too much salt water with their seafood.

Some black bears are actually white. No, they aren't polar bears—they are white black bears, called **KERMODES**. The phenomenon is caused by a particular combination of genes. You can find these white kermode bears in special places along the B.C. coast.

Ever since I was a cub I've felt, somehow, different.

What eating habits! **MOOSE** (and deer, elk, and other animals called ruminants) burp up food from their stomachs to chew and swallow again. Why? Those woody twigs are tough to digest the first time. So a moose will bring them up for another good chew, then swallow them into its second stomach this time. Did I mention that moose have four stomachs?

Isn't that how everybody eats?

BEAVERS alter the environment more than any other mammal except—guess who?—humans. It's because of all those dams and ponds they construct. Since a beaver's teeth never stop growing, it needs to gnaw on wood to keep them trimmed. (If you gnawed on wood as much as a beaver does, your teeth would be worn down to nothing.)

Another neat thing about beavers: they have special see-through eyelids (like built-in goggles) so they can see under water. And they can also close a small flap to prevent water from getting up their nostrils when they swim.

Racoons love city living. Toronto has the densest population of racoons anywhere in Canada.

The **ATLANTIC GIANT SQUID** has the largest eyes of any animal. According to the Guinness Book of Records, the record-breaker was a giant squid found in Thimble Tickle Bay, Newfoundland, in 1878. Its eyes were about fifty centimetres across, which is the diameter of a car tire.

Eat your milkweed so you grow big and toxic.

MONARCH CATERPILLARS are huge eaters! In two weeks, a newly hatched monarch caterpillar eats so much milkweed that it balloons to 3,000 times its birthweight. If an average-sized human baby grew at the same rate, it would weigh nine tons (the weight of two elephants) at the end of the two weeks. You might think a nice, fat, juicy caterpillar would be a tasty morsel for other animals. Think again. Monarch caterpillars store poison from the milkweed plant in their bodies, making them lethal to predators.

Did you know that **BATS'** knees bend backwards? And did you also know why bats hang out upside down? They can't stand up! (Their skinny legs, made lightweight for flying, can't support their bodies.)

OWLS can't move their eyes from side to side. But they can turn their heads 270 degrees to either side and tilt them completely upside down.

Owls also have awesome hearing. They can pinpoint where a noise is coming from and hear a mouse step on a twig twenty-five metres away. One ear points forward and slightly up, while the other points down and towards the back of the head. An owl's face is bowl-shaped, like a satellite dish, to better receive sound waves.

FALCONS can reach 180 kilometres an hour in a dive. A falcon will swoop up on its prey from behind, hit it with its feet, then sweep back to catch the stunned prey. If the dinner is not dead from the initial impact, the falcon uses its beak to snap its neck.

Hold the myth! **LEMMINGS** do not deliberately plunge over cliffs to their deaths. Lemmings do have population explosions every few years, though, which means their living conditions become so crowded that some are forced to depart in search of new homes. It's a hazardous journey through unfamiliar territory. But if the lemmings fall over cliffs or swim out to sea and drown during their voyage, that's accidental. More likely, they'll die by becoming breakfast for a predator.

Peculiar Plants: No Picking!

Plants Are Particularly Peculiar

Some plants like it hot. Some like it cold. Some like it wet. Fortunately, Canada is big enough and diverse enough to practically have it all, so there's a huge variety of plants growing in this land. Here are a few particularly peculiar specimens.

BENT OUT OF SHAPE

The trees that grow out of cracks in the Niagara Escarpment have had a tough life. You'd be stunted, gnarled, bent, and scraggly, too, if you spent all your time in blasting winds and freezing winters.

The Niagara Escarpment is a line of rocky cliffs that stretches across southern Ontario. The trees growing there may not look too impressive, but show some respect! They are hundreds, or even a thousand, years old. This is actually an old-growth forest. The reason it's not very big is that the trees grow slowly. According to the Guinness Book of Records, one of these trees holds the world record for slow growth. After 155 years, it was only 10.2 centimetres tall, less than the height of a can of pop.

If you cut one down (please don't!), you would probably need a microscope to count the annual growth rings because they're crowded so closely together. A tree with a trunk that's the diameter of a baseball, for example, might have as many as 500 rings.

DRUNKEN FOREST

Sometimes trees growing in the subarctic can't stand up straight, so these northern forests are called drunken forests. Underneath the shallow layer of soil, the ground is permanently frozen. The tree roots can't penetrate deeply enough to hold the trees firmly upright—so they keel over.

YOU ATE THAT!

This news may shock you: you've probably eaten seaweed!

Irish moss, a purplish seaweed, is harvested from the sea and shoreline off Prince Edward Island. People buy it and use the jelly-like substance it produces to thicken liquids or make food ingredients stay together. Adding some Irish moss can prevent the chocolate in chocolate milk from sinking to the bottom, make ice cream creamy, help whipped cream hold its shape, and thicken toothpaste. It's even found in jelly beans!

Hey! When you look closely, Irish moss looks like lots of tiny moose antlers.

SOME LIKE IT HOT

Smokey the Bear, take note: forest fires are not always bad for the forest.

A lodgepole pine has cones that are sealed shut with a glue-like resin. Some of these cones will open only when they're exposed to tremendous heat— such as the heat caused by a forest fire. After a fire, the cones open and release their seeds. The timing is perfect. You see, the fire has also prepared the ground for planting by burning off grasses and fertilizing with ash.

Wait a minute! What if there are no forest fires for several years? Don't worry. Not all the cones of the lodgepole pine need great heat to open. It holds some in reserve for those fire-free years.

Treemendous trees grow on Canada's mild, Wet Coast. Er... I mean West Coast. Where it's very west— I mean wet. That's why the trees grow so big.

Some trees on the West Coast are more than a thousand years old and as high as a twenty-storey apartment building!

This is quite the rainforest.

PHEW!

What looks like a big cabbage but smells like a skunk? Skunk cabbage, of course. This stinky plant has the largest leaves of any plant native to Canada. Think of the cabbage rolls you could make with leaves a metre long and half a metre wide.

As for the smell, some insects like it, and deer and bear are among those who think skunk cabbages taste just fine.

MISPLACED FOREST

It's ridiculous to think of a lush, swampy forest way up in the High Arctic, near the North Pole. Forests can't grow in the Arctic. It's too cold and dry, right?

Right! But wrong too. Scientists on Canada's northernmost island, Axel Heiberg, are studying the fossilized stumps and leaves of a forest that actually grew there 45 million years ago. At that time, the climate was much warmer. There were even alligators there!

Tread Carefully: Dirty Tricks and Wild Shenanigans Ahead

Strange Goings-on in the Wilds of Canada

Some very weird things happen when plants and animals get together—cheating, dirty tricks, and even secret underground deals. Here's a peek at some of this outrageous behaviour.

CHEATERS

Don't be fooled by the flowers on the lady's slipper orchid. They look beautiful, but they don't play fair.

Bumblebees are attracted to the blossoms, which they think will be a source of nectar. Instead—gotcha!—the bee is caught inside a trap of petals. To escape, the insect flies towards a narrow opening in the flower. As it squishes through the gap, it ends up with a sticky mass of pollen smeared on its back. If the bee visits another lady's slipper (some bees never learn), the pollen rubs onto this second plant, fertilizing its seeds. Score one for the flowers. Meanwhile, the poor bee still hasn't found any nectar.

Sea Otter

Kelp

Lady's Slipper

Kelp! I'm lost!

The lady's slipper is the official provincial flower of Prince Edward Island.

Then it should improve its behaviour!

A TANGLED TALE OF TWO SEA CRITTERS AND A SEAWEED

Forests of slimy kelp, which is a brown seaweed, grow under water along the B.C. coast. Kelp is amazing—it can grow as tall as a tree in one summer, and it's also the largest plant in the sea. As in a forest on land, all sorts of critters shelter and feed in this ocean forest. Sea urchins like to munch on the kelp. They are such gobblers, in fact, that they would destroy the kelp forest if it weren't for the sea otters that gobble them up. It's a handy arrangement for everybody.

In the 1800s, fur traders who arrived by sailing ship on the West Coast of Canada killed hundreds of thousands of sea otters for their thick furs. With the sea otters almost wiped out, the sea urchin population boomed. Armies of urchins gobbled up the underwater kelp forests. The kelp needed help! The government brought in some surviving sea otters from Alaska to start a new B.C. population. The sea otters started eating up sea urchins, and eventually the kelp forests were able to grow back. Everybody lived happily ever after.

Clark's Nutcracker

BIRD BRAIN!

The whitebark pine tree has a dandy arrangement with the Clark's nutcracker: it gets the bird to do some of the work of planting its seeds! In the fall, the nutcracker collects seeds from the cones of the white-bark pine tree, carries them away, and buries them. One bird can cache 30,000 to 100,000 seeds! When winter comes, the nutcracker digs up the seeds and dines on them—although the bird can never find all the seeds it hid. New pine trees grow from the unde-tected seeds.

UNDERGROUND DEALS

Some of the biggest, toughest trees couldn't live without the underground deal they've made with their tiny fungal friends. Fungi (that's the plural of fun-gus) live in the forest soil. (You'll be familiar with store-bought mushrooms, which are the fruit of one kind of fungus, but there are many other kinds.) Fungi spread out a mat of fine hairs through the upper layer of the soil. When these hairs touch a tree's roots, they provide the tree with a gift—nutrients from the soil. The tree returns the favour by making sugar in its leaves, which it sends down to its roots so the fungi get their share.

Sundew

Pitcher Plant

Fungi

Flying Squirrel

Don't forget my role. I help by eating the fungi and spreading fungi spores, through my droppings, to the roots of young trees.

INSECT-EATING PLANTS

Many plants live in the bogs of Canada, but since bogs don't supply enough nutrients for all the plants, some of them are forced—like in a horror movie—to eat insects! Here are two car-nivorous culprits.

Sundews have glue-tipped tentacles that nab small insects. The more a captured insect struggles, the more entangled it gets. Then the edges of the sun-dew leaf bend slowly inward, the plant's digestive juices fin-ish off the insect, and the plant absorbs this liquid food.

Pitcher plants are shaped like open-mouthed jugs. Look inside and you'll find col-lected rainwater and decaying insects. The insects are attracted to this smelly stew, and they crawl down the sloping hairs on the inside of the jug towards the bot-tom. But the hairs prevent the insects from climbing up again. There's no escape! It's either death by drowning or slow digestion by the plant's enzymes. Some choice!

EXCEEDINGLY WEIRD

Mosses grow on moose droppings, of all places! Actually, it makes sense. Moose droppings act as fertilizer to help the new moss plants grow. But how do the tiny spores (the moss plant's seeds) end up on the drop-pings? When flies land on little umbrella-shaped landing pads on the moss, the spores there stick to their feet. The flies then carry them to the moose droppings—air express!

Two-legged Visitors Arriving

Chapter 3

O Canada: Who Was Here First, and Who Came Next

Jump on board—we're setting sail for the past. You haven't seen history like this before! Thousands of years of traditional Native life in what we now call Canada will be interrupted when strange newcomers in funny hats arrive in sailing ships. Be ready for anything. We're going exploring!

Savvy livin' off the land

Surviving in the Arctic

Explorers who accidentally bumped into North America

Getting lost, getting stuck, and getting scurvy

Arctic ho! More to explore

Travels by land though mosquito-infested bogs and canoe-crunching rivers

Fearsome fights and battles

Taming the Wild West

Do you think you should bring a cellphone?

Get on board. We're going exploring!

Like the early European explorers who sailed across the Atlantic Ocean and discovered North America?

Right! We'll find new lands, things never before encountered. Treasure!

We'd better take a lunch. We'll also need some navigational instruments so we don't get lost.

Maybe we should bring a map too.

Explorers don't have maps. They make maps after they discover what's there.

Well, if we're lost, can we ask people we meet for directions?

Sure we can. The European explorers got a lot of help from the Native people who were already living in North America. And not just about where to go, but also about how to survive in the wilderness.

Well, shall we set off?

Actually, I'm getting kind of hungry. Maybe we should have lunch first.

Good plan. We'll eat oranges rich in vitamin C. We don't want to get scurvy on the long voyage. Over lunch you can tell me more about those explorers from long ago. Maybe I can pick up a few exploring tips. By the way, do you think we should phone ahead and tell the people we're going to discover that we'll be arriving?

So they aren't surprised?

So they can put out some snacks. It could be a matter of survival. Explorers get hungry, you know.

Anybody home?

35

Here First

Full speed reverse! We're backing up hundreds, even thousands, of years. We'll check out the scene—the *prehistorical* scene—in what we now call Canada long before Europeans arrived. Contrary to what some of them liked to think, Canada was not a *terra nullius* (empty land) before they got here.

WHO WERE THE FIRST NATIONS?

People from many different Native nations lived in Canada for thousands of years before Europeans even knew this land existed. These people didn't keep written records, so we don't know as much about them as we would like. What we do know is that they spoke more than fifty different languages, they traded with each other and formed alliances, and they sometimes warred with each other.

These aboriginal people developed a lifestyle that fit their environment—whether that environment was coastal, forest, tundra, or grassland. They speared salmon, planted corn, paddled skin-covered canoes, hunted buffalo, and built houses out of snow. They had ceremonies and sacred quests, and they called on spirits from the natural world for assistance and protection. They told stories as a way of passing their beliefs and their knowledge of earlier events from one generation to the next. They had rich cultures and traditions based on their ties to the land. Their way of life lasted for thousands of years.

It would change forever when newcomers arrived from Europe.

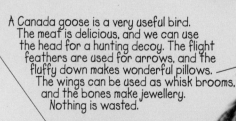

A Canada goose is a very useful bird.
The meat is delicious, and we can use
the head for a hunting decoy. The flight
feathers are used for arrows, and the
fluffy down makes wonderful pillows.
The wings can be used as whisk brooms,
and the bones make jewellery.
Nothing is wasted.

Very interesting.
Gotta go now.
Urgent appointment
somewhere else.

BUFFALO HUNT

Hear the rumble! Feel the ground shake! Incoming buffalo!

Enormous herds of buffalo—tens of thousands of huge, hairy animals—used to thunder across the open grasslands of the prairies. But it's hard to steer stampeding buffalo in the direction you want them to go. So Plains Natives worked as a team to direct such herds between large stone cairns, or mounds. The cairns were arranged to form a V-shape that pointed towards a cliff, the buffalo jump. Forward momentum propelled the animals over the edge and to the ground below, where young men with spears finished them off.

A dead buffalo was like a department store for the First Nations. It provided food, clothing, and shelter. Tools could be made from bone, cups and spoons from horns, a water bag from the stomach, glue from the hoofs—even the dung could be burned for fuel.

SAILING AWAY

The West Coast people used enormous cedar trees to build large carved and wonderfully decorated canoes. An ocean-going canoe made from a single tree could be as long as the European sailing ships the First Nations later encountered. Loaded with supplies and as many as seventy people, a canoe could travel hundreds of kilometres.

ROCK SMARTS

Early aboriginals chipped and shaped rock to form arrowheads, scrapers, knives—all their essential hunting weapons and dandy kitchen implements. But not just any old rock would do. To create a sharp cutting edge, the rock had to be hard and fine-grained, such as flint, chert, quartzite, or a black volcanic glass called obsidian.

LOOK BACK! WAAAAY BACK!

Archaeologists on the coast of Labrador have found a child's grave that was dug more than 7,000 years ago. Seven thousand years! That's way before the Egyptian pyramids were built or the wheel was invented.

The twelve-year-old child in the grave was buried with great care. He (actually, scientists don't know if it was a boy or a girl) is lying on his front, his head turned to the side, surrounded by various offerings: a walrus tusk, spear points, a pendant made of bone, and a whistle made of bird bone. A big pile of stones and boulders covered the grave.

Who was this child, and why was he given such a fancy burial? Nobody knows. The large, elaborate grave under the boulder pile at L'Anse-Amour in Labrador is the oldest such grave found anywhere in the world.

EXCEEDINGLY WEIRD

Some of the food treats eaten by aboriginal people in years past may seem a little strange to us today. The Huron, for example, farmers who lived around the Great Lakes, would soak small, immature ears of corn in a pond until they fermented. Yummy!

A special Cree treat was beaver tail. And if the family had recently caught a moose, you might be offered some of the tastiest parts of the animal—the bone marrow and the nose.

FASHION SENSE

You can't survive a Canadian winter without warm clothing. But aboriginal people couldn't buy their wardrobes off the rack at the mall, so they made their own.

Hold on before you sew! Animal skins have to be processed before they are soft enough to make into clothing. If they aren't, the skins will dry as stiff as a board. You need to know how to scrape and work the skins, and how to break down the fibres that make them stiff, perhaps with urine, animal fat, or a paste made of animal brains. Then you'll need to clean, dry, smoke, and soften the skins. *Now* you can sew!

Arctic Living

Head north—but bring your woollies! The Arctic was (and is) home to the Inuit, a people with amazing thermal smarts. They needed these skills to survive in a land where firewood was scarce (too cold for trees!) and winters were unbelievably frigid, dark, and l-o-o-o-o-o-ng.

THERE'S SNOW PLACE LIKE HOME

Consider the igloo! Is this an ingenious idea or what?

In the Arctic, there's no wood to build houses, but there is snow. The Inuit knew exactly what kind of wind-packed snow was best for cutting into blocks with saw-toothed caribou antlers. These blocks would then be placed on top of each other and shaped into a sturdy dome. (A dome is a very secure and spacious structure.) The rounded shape of the igloo also cleverly sheds blasts from winter storms. (That's why many camping tents are dome-shaped today.) What's more, snow contains trapped air, making it a great insulating material. The heat of the human bodies in the igloo, along with the flame from a small oil lamp, is enough to keep it warm. (Well, warm enough for survival anyway.)

Some igloos even had windows! The builders used a sheet of ice or a piece of semi-transparent seal intestine with a peephole cut in the middle.

FROZEN MYSTERY

Here's an Arctic mystery from the depths of time. Where did the Dorset people go? When the ancestors of today's Inuit arrived in the Arctic about a thousand years ago, there were already other people living there. The Dorset people (also called the Tunit people) had lived there for at least 3,000 years. Then they vanished. Archaeologists have unearthed the remains of their camps, as well as many delightful tiny carvings they made, often of polar bears. But where did the Dorset go? Were they killed or driven away? Did they mix with the Inuit and adopt their ways? It's a mystery, and it happened so long ago that we may never know.

Can you make those out of sealskin?

We're off to hunt bowhead whales! We're paddling an umiak made from sealskin. Some umiaks also have sails made from seal intestines! We have harpoons made from bone, and floats made of inflated sealskin.

Do you have government-approved personal flotation devices?

Ummmm. Cozy!

CUSTOM-MADE FOR THE COLD

The Inuit made particularly high-quality winter wear. Using a special tight lockstitch, they sewed caribou skins with bone needles and thread made from wet sinews (tissues) taken from the animal's back and legs. As the sinews dried and shrank, the garment's seams became watertight.

Cool shades!

We carved snow goggles to protect our eyes from the glare of the sun on the snow.

GO THAT-A-WAY

It's hard to find your way across snow-covered tundra in a blizzard. Every which way is white. That's why the Inuit constructed stone cairns called Inuksuk (which means "that which stands for a man"). Some Inuksuk really do look like stone men. They were built to mark travel routes, indicate good kayak-launching sites, and for many other purposes. Some, with sprigs of heather sticking out and flapping in the wind, acted like scarecrows to herd caribou towards the hunting grounds.

WHAT'S FOR DINNER?

What about an Inuit treat of seal intestines and stomachs stuffed with partly digested shrimp? Lichens, which are not normally edible, are scrumptious when pulled from the stomach of freshly killed caribou. Arctic char can be stored in cool rock caches until the fish has acquired the taste and feel of old cheese. Mmm!

Careful when you turn the page! The aboriginal people are about to make contact with people from a very different culture, with different beliefs, different languages, and different behaviours. Does this sound like a recipe for trouble?

COMPANY'S COMING

These Things Happen When You Go Exploring

We're sailing away to discover the New World. We'll find a shortcut to China and become rich and famous. We'll claim new lands for our king.

Or maybe we'll be gobbled by sea monsters. We'll hit an iceberg or get lost. We'll get scurvy, have our gums rot and our teeth fall out.

You never know what will happen when you go exploring.

VIKINGS IN NEWFOUNDLAND

In 1960, archaeologists poking about a cove at the northern tip of Newfoundland found some grassy mounds. Big deal, right? But wait a second—those bumpy humps turned out to be the overgrown remains of a thousand-year-old Norse settlement.

Revise the history books! Boot Christopher Columbus off his pedestal! There's a new winner in the race to be the first Europeans in North America! This Norse site is the earliest evidence of European settlement on this continent. (Of course, Native people were living here long before that.)

Old Icelandic sagas (or stories) tell of Lief the Lucky, who sailed in a wooden boat from Greenland across the treacherous ocean to a place called Vinland. Over the years, various people have suggested different locations for this legendary place. Could it be here, in this rocky cove in Newfoundland? Maybe. Then again, maybe not. Maybe we'll never know.

SHORTCUT TO CHINA

Many explorers dreamed of finding a new route to China, with its rich silks and spices. Once they discovered that the New Land (later called North America) was blocking their way, they looked for a way around or through this obstacle. They had no idea how big it really was! They tried sailing farther north and farther south. They even tried going around the top, looking for a passage through the Arctic from the Atlantic to the Pacific.

JOHN CABOT WAS HERE (WHERE?)

John Cabot sailed from England in 1497, looking for a route to China. When he found North America instead, he went ashore and claimed the land for England.

It's too bad Cabot didn't write his name in a visitors' book somewhere, for today nobody knows for sure exactly where he landed. Was it Newfoundland? Or perhaps farther south, in the United States? Unfortunately, we can't ask Cabot. He set off on another voyage the following year, and nothing was ever heard of him again.

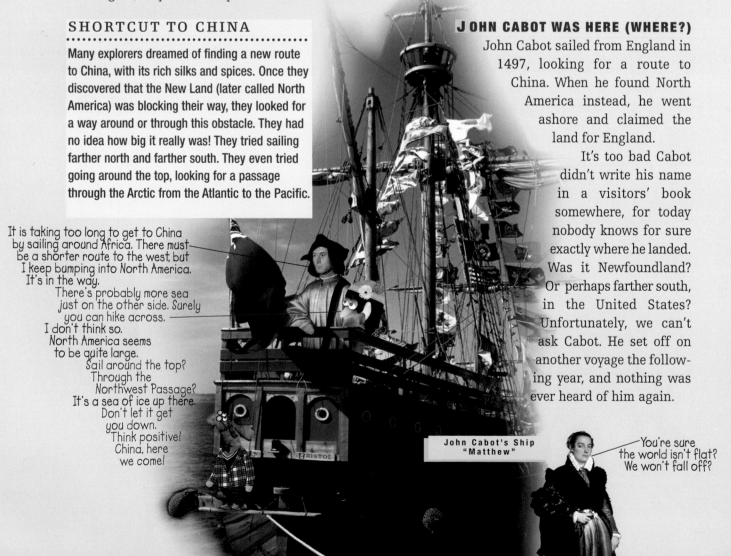

It is taking too long to get to China by sailing around Africa. There must be a shorter route to the west, but I keep bumping into North America. It's in the way.

There's probably more sea just on the other side. Surely you can hike across.

I don't think so. North America seems to be quite large.

Sail around the top? Through the Northwest Passage? It's a sea of ice up there. Don't let it get you down. Think positive! China, here we come!

John Cabot's Ship "Matthew"

BRISTOL

You're sure the world isn't flat? We won't fall off?

CLAIM YOUR LAND FOR THE KING OF FRANCE!

What nerve! The French explorer Jacques Cartier had an attitude typical of many Europeans at the time. He figured that North America was free for the taking, and so were the people living there!

Cartier first sailed to North America in 1534. He was looking for a route to China, of course. And although he didn't find it, he did meet various First Nations people. One of these was Donnacona, the chief of the Stadacona people (their village was where Quebec City is today).

Cartier encountered Donnacona and his people on the shore of the Gaspé, where they had gone in their canoes to fish. In the presence of the Stadacona chief, Cartier erected a nine-metre-high wooden cross to claim the land for France. "*Vive le Roi de France!*" (Long live the king of France), read the words on the cross. Donnacona figured out what the words meant, and he became angry. But Cartier pretended the cross was just a landmark so he would be able to find his way back again. A likely story!

When he sailed home, Cartier took with him Donnacona's two sons. Souvenirs of the trip! He returned them, as promised, when he came back to explore the St. Lawrence River the following year, 1535. However, before Cartier sailed back to France *again*, he seized Donnacona and seven others, recaptured his sons, and took everyone back with him. Donnacona desperately wanted to return home, but he and his fellow captives died in France a few years later.

This is *Samuel de Champlain's* statue in Ottawa. He went exploring up the Ottawa River in 1613. What's he holding? An astrolabe. It's an instrument the early explorers used to figure out where they were.

Too bad he's holding it upside down.

SET SAIL

Meanwhile, on the Other Side of the Continent ...

Never give up! When the European explorers failed to find a handy water route through North America from the Atlantic Ocean, they started exploring along the Pacific. They met the local Natives, collected a ton of sea otter pelts, and ventured up a lot of inlets hoping to find the western entrance to that elusive Northwest Passage. Darn it, foiled again!

PSSSST! DON'T TELL THE SPANISH!

The great English explorer Sir Francis Drake probably made a secret exploration of the coast of British Columbia way back in 1579. New evidence suggests that he sailed as far north as the Queen Charlotte Islands that year. But Drake's crew had to swear on pain of death not to tell where they had been, and maps of the expedition were drawn incorrectly to disguise how far up the coast Drake had sailed.

Sir Francis Drake

Top Secret

It was all hush-hush because Drake believed he had found the other end of (guess what?) the Northwest Passage. He didn't want the Spanish, who were also exploring the Pacific coast, to know.

As a result of all this sneaky stuff, historians have uncovered evidence of this mysterious 1579 voyage only recently. They had thought the first European explorers reached this part of the B.C. coast in the 1700s. Now it looks as if they were poking about 200 years earlier!

(Remember, if the king of Spain asks you about Drake's trip, you don't know anything.)

NOOTKA BEFORE YOU SMASH INTO THOSE ROCKS!

Look out! Captain Cook's ship, *Resolution*, was sailing up the west coast of Vancouver Island in 1778 when it ventured too close to a reef. The aboriginal inhabitants of a nearby village called out, *"Nutka, itchme!"* which means, roughly, "Go around that way." But Cook thought Nootka was their name, so that's what he called them. Everyone who came after Cook did too.

Nootka, schmootka! The Nootka actually called themselves the Mowachaht (people of the deer), and their village was called Yuquot (where the wind blows from all directions).

Got it, Cap'n?

(P.S. Cook also goofed when he claimed the Mowachaht's territory for the king of England. The Mowachaht weren't giving it away.)

MUCH MUSIC

When Captain Cook sailed into Nootka Sound, on what's now Vancouver Island, the local people paddled their canoes out in welcome. Later they sang songs that were "by no means unpleasant to the Ear," according to one crew member. In return, the men on board played a tune with the fife and drum (a fife is like a small flute). After the locals sang another song, the sailors then entertained them with French horns!

Captain Cook

I thought Captain Cook had a hook on his hand. You know, like in that story about Peter Pan?

That was Captain Hook. This is Cook. You are mistook!

THE CAPTURE OF JOHN JEWITT

John Jewitt, a nineteen-year-old American blacksmith, was captured by Chief Maquinna at Nootka Sound in 1803. Maquinna had been trading with Jewitt's ship, but he became very angry when the American captain insulted him. In retaliation, he and his men seized the ship, beheading twenty-five crew members. Jewitt was spared because he could repair muskets and make knives.

For almost three years, Jewitt lived with Maquinna and his people, learning their language, dressing like them, and even taking a wife (he was threatened with death if he didn't). He began to understand and respect his captors. He even recognized that often it was the behaviour of the European traders that provoked Native attacks such as the one on his ship.

Although Jewitt was treated well by the Mowachaht, it was not his choice to stay. He had almost given up hope of leaving when another American ship sailed into the bay. Maquinna wanted to trade with the ship, and he told Jewitt to write a letter he could take to the ship's captain. Jewitt wrote the letter, but he betrayed the chief by asking that Maquinna be captured and held in irons so Jewitt would be released. When Jewitt finally stepped aboard the ship, the captain was amazed. He was wearing bearskins, his face and body were painted red and black, and his hair, which had not been cut for more than two years, was piled on his head and held with a spruce twig.

Jewitt persuaded the captain to let Maquinna go. In his diary, the American later described saying goodbye to his former captor: "I could not avoid experiencing a painful sensation on parting with this savage chief, who had preserved my life, and in general treated me with kindness."

EXCEEDINGLY WEIRD

What must the Native inhabitants of North America have thought when they first saw Europeans? These strangers had beards! They had magic sticks that exploded with a big bang! Were they strange beings from the moon?

The people made up various names for these newcomers. One name meant "suddenly, they're there." Another meant "people who live in a boat." Another was "metal people" (because the Europeans brought metal things to trade).

The Mowachaht tell stories of what their ancestors thought the first time they saw a European ship. They noticed that one sailor had a hooked nose and another had a hunchback. To the Mowachaht, these sailors resembled a dog salmon and a humpback salmon. The Natives thought Captain Cook's ship was "a fish come alive into people."

Exceedingly weird!

Exceedingly weird!

Icebergs Ahead

Arctic Exploration: To Find the Northwest Passage

Journey to the ends of the earth! Like today's astronauts blasting off into unknown space, Arctic explorers sailed into treacherous, ice-choked waters, never knowing what lay ahead. Why? To find the Northwest Passage, that's why!

SO LONG, CAP'N HUDSON

In 1611, the British explorer Henry Hudson figured he had found the Northwest Passage. (Yeah, right!) Actually he was stuck in Hudson Bay. His starving, frostbitten crew wanted to go home, but Hudson was determined to stay and find the real Northwest Passage. The crew mutinied. They put Hudson, his teenage son, John, and all those who were sick with scurvy into a small boat and set it adrift in the mist. The others sailed home, and Hudson was never seen again.

SCURVY AND OTHER DELIGHTS OF FOREIGN TRAVEL

Exploring can be hazardous to your health! British expedition leaders usually hired twice as many sailors as they needed, figuring that half would die on the voyage. Often, they died of scurvy.

Scurvy is caused by a lack of vitamin C (found in fresh fruits and vegetables). Victims' gums bleed and rot, their teeth fall out, their swollen legs become covered with purple blotches, their joints ache, they lose weight, they're exhausted, and eventually they die.

Captain Cook made his crew eat a special diet that included onions, malt, sauerkraut, salted cabbage, carrot marmalade, and various grasses. The crew hated the stuff, but Captain Cook told them to eat it or get a lashing. (And you thought *your* parents were strict?) The crew members did as they were told. Cook wrote, "For the first time in recorded history of a long sea voyage, not one man was lost from scurvy."

I don't want scurvy.
Then eat your veggies.
I hate veggies.
Okay, how about eating the half-digested stomach contents of a caribou? That's what the Inuit sometimes ate to prevent scurvy.
Blech!
It's all a matter of taste.
You know what? My vegetables don't taste so bad any more.

LOOKING FOR CHINA? TAKE THIS ROUTE

I goofed! I thought I found the Northwest Passage, but it turns out I didn't.

I made a wrong turn into Hudson Bay.

Sixty-one out of my sixty-four men died of extreme cold and scurvy.

I got shipwrecked and was never seen again.

All that darned ice in the way!

Martin Frobisher
1576–78

Henry Hudson
1610–11

Jens Munk
1619–20

James Knight
1719

Edward Parry
1819

LOST: JOHN FRANKLIN. REWARD.

What happened to Sir John Franklin? It's one of the greatest mysteries in Canadian history.

Franklin's expedition sailed from England in 1845 in search of the Northwest Passage. But the 129 men in the crew disappeared off the face of the earth! What went wrong? Over the next ten years, forty expeditions went looking for clues. (They mapped a lot of the Arctic while they were at it.)

Some searchers encountered Inuit carrying silver forks and spoons from Franklin's ships. These Inuit told stories of white men walking south and dropping from starvation. A bleached skeleton, dressed in fragments of a uniform, was found on King William Island, in today's Nunavut. A note inside a rock cairn, apparently written more than two years into the expedition, said that the ships had been crushed in the ice and twenty-four men, including John Franklin, were dead. The 105 survivors were walking south, according to the note, hoping eventually to reach the nearest fur-trade fort. They were dragging heavy lifeboats on sledges, one of which was later discovered by searchers. It was filled with supplies (including silk handkerchiefs and button polish!) and two human skeletons.

EXCEEDINGLY WEIRD

How could things have gone so wrong for the Franklin expedition? Recently, chilling new evidence has been uncovered. In 1986, scientists received permission to examine the bodies of three crew members who had died during the expedition's first winter. Their graves were found on windswept Beechley Island. The bodies were amazingly well preserved in the frozen ground. They showed evidence of pneumonia, tuberculosis, and scurvy.

The surprising news was that their bodies also contained extremely high levels of lead. This lead, which can be toxic in large quantities, would have slowly poisoned them, making them weak and exhausted, and contributing to their deaths. It would even have affected their minds, making them act strangely.

Where did the lead come from? The Franklin crew brought with them the latest in food-preservation technology —tin cans! In tin cans, fresh food could be stored indefinitely. This could prevent scurvy, the scourge of long voyages. There were 8,000 tin cans on board the Franklin expedition's ships, but the lids and seams of each one were sealed shut with solder, a mixture of lead and tin. They were a deadly time bomb.

It's likely that as the men ate the canned food, thinking they were keeping themselves healthy, they were being slowly poisoned by the lead.

I was marooned in the Arctic for four years until rescued by a whaling ship!

Sir John Ross
1829

We never returned. My wife sent out search parties.

John Franklin
1845

I found it! I found the Northwest Passage! (Does anyone still care?)

Roald Amundsen
1905

I'm travelling through the Northwest Passage with an ice-breaker escort. I have radar, sonar, GPS, satellite communications, up-to-the-minute weather updates, downloadable satellite photos showing iceberg locations ...

Goose
2002

No Couch Potatoes Beyond This Point

Exploring Canada by Land (Are We There Yet?)

Let's explore overland, trekking or canoeing across the vast continent! We'll go north. We'll go west. We'll find new sources of furs. We'll discover a river leading to a western sea (that will be our route to China). We've even heard of mountains made of gold!

Of course, we don't have maps, and we don't know where the heck we're going. We'd never survive in the wilderness on our own. No problem. The Natives know this country well. We'll take a guided tour!

Next time, I'm travelling by snowmobile.

Samuel Hearne

TOENAIL-DESTROYING TREK

Samuel Hearne trekked overland from Hudson Bay across the northern Barren Lands to the Arctic Ocean—and back! More than 5,600 kilometres. The Hudson's Bay Company explorer was looking for a route to the Western Sea. He had also heard that there was copper in the North.

Hearne's first two attempts ended in disaster when he was robbed and left to starve by his Native guides. Lucky for him, he was rescued by the respected Chipewyan chief Matonabbee.

With Matonabbee leading the way, Hearne started out again with a Chipewyan party in December 1770. Over trackless wastes. Cold, wet, and hungry. They followed the seasonal caribou migrations, then headed down the Coppermine River to the Arctic Ocean. His travelling companions massacred a party of Inuit (their traditional enemies) on the Coppermine, and they were disgusted when Hearne wouldn't join them.

When Hearne reached the Arctic Ocean, he wondered why he had bothered. It was choked with ice and useless as a route to the Western Sea. Not only that, but he found just one measly lump of copper!

Hearne lost his toenails to frostbite on the long, exhausting trek back to Hudson Bay. He arrived back more than a year after he had left, having travelled farther north than any other European.

WILDERNESS TIPS

The European explorers faced incredible challenges while they were travelling through the Canadian wilderness. The success or failure of an expedition often depended on the First Nations guides. The guides had travelled the same routes many times before, and they knew how to survive in the wilderness and could act as interpreters with other Native groups.

What a trip, eh?
And imagine losing your toenails!
I don't have toenails.
Nor did Samuel Hearne—
after that trip.

ALEX WAS HERE

Alexander Mackenzie was looking for a land route across Canada to the Pacific Ocean. From there, he believed, it would be a short sail to China. The first river he followed ended up at the Arctic Ocean instead. Darn it! Mackenzie named the river the River of Disappointment. (It's now called the Mackenzie.)

If at first you don't succeed … Mackenzie set off again in a large canoe with his guides and some voyageurs—and a friendly dog. This time, after a typically death-defying journey through canoe-crunching rapids, followed by a treacherous hike on foot along a First Nations grease trail (along which they would carry eulachon oil for trade) through the mountains, he arrived at the Pacific Ocean near Bella Coola. Hurrah! The date was July 22, 1793. We know that because Mackenzie scrawled a message with the date on a big rock where he camped.

47

Fearsome Fights and Battles

Grab your tomahawk! Load your musket! Prepare for war!

We're off to some of the fierce fights, bloody battles, and historical dust-ups that are part of Canada's history. Don't worry—we'll tone down the violence. Rumour has it there are adults reading.

FIRST NATIONS WARFARE

Warfare was an important part of many First Nations societies. Just as we look up to sports heroes today, Native people once admired warriors who earned success in battle.

Young men trained to become skilled warriors, and long-standing feuds between nations could go on for generations. Since every killing required revenge, the fighting never ended.

The arrival of the Europeans usually made these rivalries worse. The stakes were higher because with the fur trade, there was more wealth to be won or lost. And now there were guns!

When First Nations and Métis (the children of Native and European parents) later took up arms against the European newcomers, it was usually a fight to preserve their traditional lands and way of life.

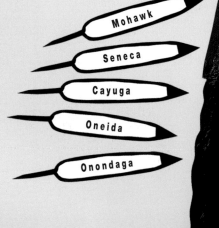

The original Five Nations of the Iroquois Confederacy

Mohawk

Seneca

Cayuga

Oneida

Onondaga

THE MIGHTY IROQUOIS CONFEDERACY

Five Iroquoian nations living south of the St. Lawrence River formed the Iroquois Confederacy, one of the most powerful, well-organized military forces in North America. Their traditional enemies were the Huron. Beginning in the early 1600s, they also had some new enemies—the Huron nation's French allies.

The most devastating attacks by Iroquois warriors began in 1648. They burned and raided Huron villages, and killed and took prisoners. Living with the Huron there were "black robes"—that's what they called the Jesuit missionaries from Europe who were attempting to persuade the Natives to become Christians—and they tortured and killed them too.

After demolishing the Huron nation, the Iroquois went after the French. Hit-and-run raids terrorized French settlers living along the St. Lawrence River. Farmers fled their fields for the protection of walled forts. Voyageurs working in the fur trade were attacked and killed or captured. The Iroquois managed to cut off the supply of furs coming to Montreal, the main source of money for the French colony.

The Iroquois raids went on for years. Finally, in 1701, the Iroquois Confederacy negotiated a peace pact with New France. Phew!

Chief Pontiac

ATTACK BY LACROSSE BALL

They shoot, they score!

Chief Pontiac led an alliance of the First Nations living around the Great Lakes. In 1763, they launched a five-week reign of terror against the British. They captured a dozen forts in bloody raids, killing more than 2,000 people and causing the British army to retreat from their lands. The First Nations were angry because Britain, having defeated New France, was now imposing its rule on them and their lands. "You have conquered the French. You have not conquered us. We are not your slaves," the Native people told the British.

In one clever assault, Sauk warriors distracted the sentries at Fort Michilmackinac, on Lake Huron, by playing lacrosse. When the ball "accidentally" sailed over the walls, the Sauk chased it inside—grabbing their weapons on the way in. The fort was captured!

Eventually, the First Nations made peace with the British, and a royal proclamation recognized their rights to a huge area of so-called Indian Territory.

GERM WARFARE

Dirty fighting! While battling Chief Pontiac's First Nations alliance, the British resorted to germ warfare. Gen. Jeffrey Amherst, the commander-in-chief of the British army in North America, ordered that blankets infected with smallpox be taken to the Native villages. Soon after the blankets arrived, the First Nations communities were devastated by a bout of the disease.

BATTLE OF THE OLDMAN

The great prairie buffalo herds started shrinking in the 1860s. Cree hunters rode farther and farther west in search of more, into Blackfoot territory. That angered the Blackfoot, destroying the long friendship that had existed between the two nations. They were now at war.

The new enemies met beside the Oldman River, in Blackfoot land. The Cree outnumbered the Blackfoot; however, the Blackfoot had rifles and shot at their rivals. Then they rushed across the river and surrounded the remaining Cree, killing hundreds.

This was the last battle between the prairie nations. The people of the buffalo, already weakened by diseases introduced by the Europeans, could not afford to fight one another. They needed to pool their remaining strength to face new threats to their land posed by European settlers.

LOG-ROLLING DEFENCE

Don't try this on your fort at home!

The legendary West Coast Tsimshian warrior Nekt defended Kitwanga Fort (near the Skeena River in northwest British Columbia, between the present-day towns of Terrace and Hazelton) against encroaching clans. The fort stood on Battle Hill and was surrounded by a fence made of spiked logs. More huge logs were hoisted up these walls and tied at the top with cedar ropes. When war horns blew, signalling an enemy attack, look out below! The logs were released to roll down and crush the invaders.

Do people still get smallpox? Not today. We developed vaccines, and the disease has virtually disappeared.

Police: Just Over the Page

49

Call in the Mounties

Welcome to the Wild West! Saddle your horse and gallop across the tall-grass prairie, where the buffalo roam (or used to). This home of the Plains First Nations is changing rapidly. Outlaws with guns and whisky are sneaking up from south of the border, the buffalo are disappearing, railways are pushing west, and homesteaders are following the railway and settling on the land. It's a rough, tough neighbourhood. Someone call the cops!

BRINGING LAW AND ORDER TO THE CANADIAN WEST

In the 1870s, American outlaws and whisky traders on the prairies gave cheap "rotgut" whisky to the Natives in return for valuable buffalo robes and other goods. It was a bad scene—then it got worse. In 1873, a party of drunken whisky traders attacked a band of Assiniboine, whom they believed had stolen some of their horses. The Americans shot thirty-six Assiniboine and burned down their village. This event became known as the Cypress Hills massacre.

The lawlessness had to be stopped! The government created the North-West Mounted Police (which later became the RCMP) to keep order. The Mounties marched in, and the outlaw traders took off.

THE RED RIVER AND NORTH-WEST REBELLIONS

These rebellions, fifteen years apart, were born of desperation. Life was becoming harder and harder in the 1800s for prairie First Nations and Métis. Native people were dying of smallpox, a railway was being constructed across the prairies, and settlers were moving onto the land. Even the buffalo herds were disappearing.

The Métis, who depended on buffalo hunting, feared that they would lose their lands, their homes, their French language, and their livelihood. They had no say in any of this! So under their leader, Louis Riel, they set up their own government and prepared to battle for their survival. Federal troops quashed the first rebellion, at Red River in Manitoba in 1869. But there was a second, more brutal rebellion in Saskatchewan in 1885.

What's a rebellion?
It's when you refuse to do what you're told, and you fight about it. Then you get grounded and lose your allowance, right?
In this rebellion, you get hanged.

This is the pits!
Absolutely pitiful!

Gabriel Dumont

Chief Poundmaker

Louis Riel

This is not a happy ending.

THE BATTLE OF BATOCHE

By May 1885, the rebellion was growing and threatening to take over the whole of western Canada. The Métis rebels had been joined by First Nations warriors, led by the Cree chiefs Poundmaker and Big Bear. At the Battle of Duck Lake, the North-West Mounted Police lost twelve men. The government used the new railway to send in troop reinforcements.

On May 9, the two sides faced each other at Batoche, headquarters of the rebellion. The 300 Métis and First Nations fighters, under their skilful military leader, Gabriel Dumont, hunkered down in rifle pits they had dug. They were badly outnumbered by government troops, but the rebels held out for four days, even firing nails and stones from their rifles when they ran out of bullets. In the end, the government troops won the battle, and although Gabriel Dumont escaped, Louis Riel was tried for treason and hanged.

"WE RECOMMEND MERCY..."

Not everyone agreed with the hanging of Riel. Even those on the jury that found him guilty wanted leniency. They commented: "We, on the jury, recommend mercy. The prisoner was guilty and we could not excuse his actions. But, at the same time, we felt that the government had not done its duty. It did nothing about the grievances of the Métis. If it had, there would never have been a second Riel rebellion."

WATCH
FOR
WARM, FURRY
WILDLIFE
AHEAD

Chapter 4

Canada: Now Open for Business

Canada is a land of opportunity, ripe for development. Fortunes can be made (and lost—oops!). The land is rich in furs, gold, and other valuable resources. What potential! Can you smell profit? To really reap the economic benefits of this land, however, we'll need to build railways, canals, highways, and pipelines. Grab a shovel—there's work to be done.

Unrelentingly cheerful voyageurs who paddle the Canadian wilderness

Business battles over the buck-toothed beaver

Miners who rush to find gold and strike it rich (or lose their shirts)

Railways in the most appalling places

Water staircases that allow ships to climb uphill

Concrete dams four times the height of Niagara Falls

Weird stuff like high walls, huge malls, and retractable roofs that don't work

Are you warm enough, Goose?

Snug as a bug in a rug. Or maybe a goose in a blanket!

Those Hudson's Bay blankets are warm. They were traded for furs during the fur trade.

See the smaller black stripes at the edge? They're like price tags. The number of stripes shows how many beaver pelts you would have to pay for that blanket.

I didn't pay for this blanket with beaver pelts.

No, but they did during the fur trade. Furs were like money. At a trading post, you could exchange them for metal knives, copper kettles, muskets, and wool blankets.

What did they do with all the furs?

Sold them in Europe for big bucks. Furs from Canada were in demand. Fashionable men thought felt hats made from beaver fur were very "cool."

Beavers? Buck-toothed, flat-tailed, oversized rodents?

What's wrong with beavers? Beavers are now our national symbol. On the Canadian crest! On the Canadian nickel!

Beavers, schmeevers! We should have the Canada goose as our national symbol instead.

The Furry Fur Trade

What a tail-thwapping tale! For hundreds of years, adventurous fur traders paddled canoes across the vast Canadian wilderness, through deadly rapids, mosquito-infested bogs, and all the usual stuff, in pursuit of pelts from those furry, flat-tailed critters with big buckteeth.

BEHIND THE SCENES AT THE FUR TRADE

The race is on! Who can get his hands on the most furry treasure? In the 1600s and 1700s, traders from Montreal and Hudson Bay ventured west and north into untravelled regions to find new fur supplies. First Nations trappers journeyed with their year's supply of pelts to trading posts that dotted the wilderness of what's now northern Ontario, Manitoba, Saskatchewan, and Alberta. Canoe brigades transported heavy loads along lakes and rivers—just like truckers on today's highways.

There was cutthroat competition for the best furs, and sometimes it got nasty. Traders routinely tried to cut off each other's fur supplies and sometimes raided each other's forts. They had price wars and "buy now, pay later" deals. They gave out free drinks—whatever would bring them more furs.

Money doesn't grow on trees-it grows on beavers.

GARAGE SALE FURS

Native people shook their heads in amazement. Those crazy fur traders! They would pay more for *used* furs—ones that had been well worn. That was because beaver hats were made using the inner fur of the beaver. On a used beaver skin that had been worn with its furry side turned in, the long outer hairs had already rubbed off, making it easier to get at the inner fur.

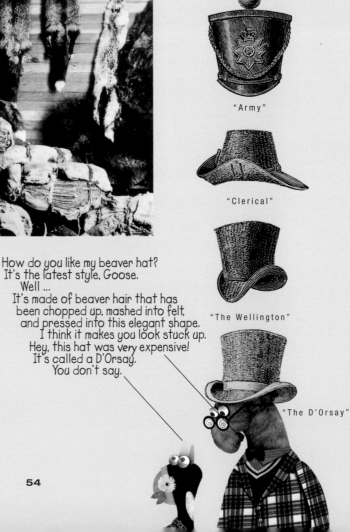

Styles of the Beaver Hat

"Continental"

"Navy"

"Army"

"Clerical"

"The Wellington"

"The D'Orsay"

How do you like my beaver hat?
It's the latest style, Goose.
Well ...
It's made of beaver hair that has been chopped up, mashed into felt, and pressed into this elegant shape.
I think it makes you look stuck up.
Hey, this hat was very expensive!
It's called a D'Orsay.
You don't say.

RADISHES AND GOOSEBERRIES

Oh, come on! Their real names weren't Radishes and Gooseberries. *Radisson* and *Des Groseilliers* were French traders and adventurers who explored the area north of Lake Superior looking for furs in the 1660s. They returned with a canoe-load of pelts and a smart business plan. Instead of bringing furs all the way south to Montreal and shipping them from there to Europe, these traders realized it would be more efficient to ship them directly from what they called the Frozen Sea (and we now call Hudson Bay).

The French just shrugged at the idea. So Radishes and Gooseberries took their plan to the English, who showed a little more enthusiasm. They particularly liked the idea of taking some of the fur trade away from the French.

In 1668, Des Groseilliers sailed to Hudson Bay in a ship called the *Nonsuch*. He traded with the Cree and returned to England with a load of the highest-quality furs. "Jolly good show!" said the English. "Let's go back for more."

And that's how the Hudson's Bay Company began.

Hey, let's not forget the real star of the fur trade!

What's it like living in Rupert's Land? Since when is this Rupert's Land? Since the king of England called it that and granted control over it to the Hudson's Bay Company. You didn't know? I guess he forgot to tell us. Funny, though, since we live here. The details are all written up here in this spiffy royal charter. Let's see ... Hey, you know what? You're not even mentioned in the charter! An oversight, I'm sure.

I'm King Charles II of England. You can call me Charlie.

The Hudson's Bay Charter 1670

GIVE ME LAND, LOTS OF LAND...

It's the big giveaway! In 1670, the king of England granted the Hudson's Bay Company a royal charter that gave it control over a huge area all around Hudson Bay. Called Rupert's Land, the area amounted to almost half of Canada!

Fur Deals, Deaths, and Dastardly Deeds

The Battle for Business

Let's hear it for the beaver. Canada was practically built on his furry little back. European traders didn't venture into the unknown northern wilderness and make contact with First Nations just to be friendly—they were looking for that buck-toothed rodent. Fortunately for the traders, the nippy northern climate just made thicker furs—and thicker furs made more money. Canada was a beaver bonanza!

You'd think they would have run out of beavers. Yes, in some areas, the supply of beavers ran out. In fact, around 1820, the Hudson's Bay Company deliberately destroyed the beaver population in the West (in what's now part of the United States) so their American rivals wouldn't get any furs. Leave no beaver alive!
Poor beavers.
Fortunately for the beavers, beaver hats eventually went out of fashion in Europe. You couldn't give away beaver pelts! So that was the end of the fur trade.

Thank goodness!

SELL YOUR FURS HERE! BEST DEALS AT THE BAY!

At first, the competition was between the British and the French. Britain shipped its furs from York Factory, on the shores of Hudson Bay, while France sent its furs by canoe to Montreal and shipped from there. Montreal was a nicer place to live than Hudson Bay, where you froze your toes for most of the year. But Hudson Bay was better for business—closer to the beaver supply.

After the British defeated the French in North America, the Hudson's Bay Company gained a new rival, the North West Company (often called the Nor'Westers). Competition was fierce! Each side would do anything—sometimes even murder!—to get more furs. Finally, in 1880, the two companies merged into one huge Hudson's Bay Company.

Today the Bay is a department-store chain where you can buy almost anything—including Hudson's Bay blankets.

THE HEAVY COST OF DOING BUSINESS

At the beginning of the fur trade, the First Nations and the Europeans were partners in business. They formed bonds of friendship and co-operation. Natives saw that they could benefit from the fur trade, so they were willing to take part. With rival trading companies competing for their furs, the First Nations had bargaining power. The European traders, meanwhile, realized that if they wanted furs, they would need to maintain good relations with their suppliers—the First Nations!

Over the years, this balance of power changed. One company—the Hudson's Bay Company—gained a monopoly over the fur trade. It could pay whatever it wanted for furs. The First Nations were weakened by diseases—and by alcohol supplied by the traders. Settlers were moving in, and the First Nations were now outnumbered in their own land. Animals they depended on, such as buffalo, were disappearing.

The fur trade brought copper kettles, muskets, and other useful metal goods to First Nations communities. But it also destroyed a traditional way of life that had endured on this continent for thousands of years.

CANADIAN VOYAGEURS.
WALKING A CANOE UP A RAPID.

UNBELIEVABLY ... AWFUL!

A terrible disease swept through the tipi camps, lodges, longhouses, and villages of Canada's Native peoples. It was a devastating, highly contagious disease, and entire communities were wiped out. Coincidentally, the disease struck shortly after the arrival of European traders and missionaries.

Of course, it was no coincidence. Europeans unknowingly brought diseases with them to North America, and smallpox was the worst. The Natives had never encountered these diseases before, so they had no resistance to them. People died by the thousands, and the Native population in North America plummeted.

57

Get Rich Quick!

Pack your grub-stake—you're going prospecting for gold. You could strike it rich! (You could lose your shirt.) Some folks have made a fortune! (Most haven't.) Better rush to the goldfields—as soon as word gets out, there will be a stampede. C'mon, take a gamble. Take a risk. Roll the dice. (Don't read the small print.) It's GOLD!

CARIBOO GOLD

In 1857, miners in California heard rumours of gold finds up north, along the banks of the Fraser River in what's now British Columbia. Thousands crammed on ships headed up the Pacific coast. Twenty-five thousand people passed through Victoria on their way to the Fraser.

Many weren't prepared for the rugged wilderness. Some drowned when their small, poorly made rafts were swamped. (They needed these rafts to get from Victoria over to the mainland, then up the Fraser.) Others froze or starved to death struggling through dense forests and over mountains. But along the banks of the Fraser, shanty towns soon sprang up, flying American flags.

Then, in 1862, Billy Barker struck it rich farther north, in the Cariboo Mountains. The second gold rush was on. Thousands of miners poured into the area, and the town of Barkerville, next to Barker's gold claim, boomed into the largest city in western Canada.

Some people became rich. Many more returned home with empty pockets. When the gold ran out, most of the miners took off for the next rush.

GO FOR THE GOLD

Whoa! Slow down! The first miners rushing to British Columbia's goldfields during the 1858 Cariboo gold rush used a rough and dangerous trail. Horses and riders frequently fell to their deaths or drowned in the swift-flowing rivers below. This was not good for business.

In 1862, engineers started replacing the trail with a wagon road up the Fraser Canyon. They had to hang down cliffs on ropes, drill holes in the rock, and set dynamite charges to blast a route. The 640-kilometre road was built almost entirely by hand, with picks and shovels. Some called the completed Cariboo Wagon Road the eighth wonder of the world. Today the Trans-Canada Highway winds along the route.

THE OVERLANDERS

You've never been on a family trip like this one! Catherine Schubert, her husband, and their three children left eastern Canada for the Cariboo goldfields in the spring of 1862. They took the train to Fort Garry (now Winnipeg). From there, they trekked across the prairies in Red River carts. They traded those in for pack horses to travel over the Rocky Mountains. Then they built rafts to float down perilous rivers. Schubert was pregnant before she left on the trip, and shortly after the family reached the goldfields, she gave birth to a baby.

THE HIKE OVER THE CHILKOOT PASS

Imagine a human chain, a never-ending line of miners trudging with back-breaking loads up a steep, snowy slope to the Chilkoot Pass. This was the thousand-metre climb from the coast into the Yukon on the usual route to the Klondike. Each person had to bring a year's worth of supplies or be turned back by the Mounties at the pass. Miners without the money to hire packers had to load up and do this hike forty times themselves! They didn't dare step out of the line because they might have to wait for hours before they could step back in again.

KLONDIKE STAMPEDE

Did you hear? A ton of gold has been discovered way up north, on Bonanza Creek in the Yukon. The 1897 Klondike gold rush was on! A hundred thousand miners started north, along with anyone else who figured he could make a buck. Most gold-seekers sailed up the Pacific coast, trudged over the mountains, built rafts to float down the Yukon River—and arrived at the boom town of Dawson, in the heart of the Klondike.

Dawson was a rowdy, rip-roaring city, with swanky hotels, swinging-door saloons, honky-tonk piano music, and can-can dancing at Diamond-Tooth Gertie's Gambling Hall.

Fifty million dollars of gold came out of the Yukon, but most people never saw any of it. Or else they spent it as soon as they got it!

WINNERS AND LOSERS

Klondike miners sometimes staked claims not knowing whether they were worth millions of bucks or zilch! A miner named William Oler figured that his claim was worthless, so he looked for a sucker to buy it. He found one—Charley Anderson was too drunk to know what he was doing when he bought Oler's claim for $800. When Anderson woke up the next morning, he tried to get his money back. The sale was legal, however, so he was stuck with the claim.

Don't feel sorry for Anderson, though. You guessed it—the mining claim he bought was worth a million dollars!

Building Railways Where No Railway Can Possibly Go

Canada is not an easy place to get around. It's big! Plus there are mountains, rivers, muskeg, and other obstacles in the way of getting anywhere.

Stay home, you suggest? Not a chance. Canadians like challenges. Challenges build character. Besides, Canadians have always had places to go, things to do, and money to make. So they have built railways to get them where they need to be!

I think I can, I think I can, I think... Uh, oh!

A RIBBON OF STEEL FROM COAST TO COAST

"A ludicrous idea!" people said in 1871. "A railway across Canada? Preposterous!"

It's hard to imagine how crazy the idea seemed at the time. Building a railway from coast to coast would be the equivalent of a trip to Mars today!

The job required thousands of labourers. They had to deal with goopy muskeg on the Canadian Shield, and they had to dodge rockfalls, avalanches, and dynamite explosions in the mountains. Construction costs went up and up. The builders kept running out of money.

But they did it! The Canadian Pacific Railway (CPR) was finally completed in 1885.

Prime Minster John A. Macdonald and his wife, Agnes, took the train trip the following year. Agnes sat on top of the cowcatcher at the front of the locomotive to get the best view of the mountains.

CAN'T GO OVER IT, GOTTA GO UNDER IT!

The ultimate challenge for the CPR builders was finding some way through B.C.'s Selkirk Mountains. The best route they could come up with was over Rogers Pass, but it was no piece of cake. On the west side of the pass, engineers had to loop the track back and forth across the valley so the trains could climb gradually to the summit. On the east side, they needed to build high trestle bridges across deep ravines. Everywhere, mud slides and avalanches poured down the steep slopes.

Those avalanches! By 1916, snow slides had killed 250 workers. Eventually, the CPR gave up and re-routed the railway through tunnels under the mountains. The Mount Macdonald Tunnel under Rogers Pass is seventeen kilometres long— making it the longest tunnel in North America.

TIGHT SQUEEZE

Andrew McCulloch, the chief engineer responsible for building the Kettle Valley Railway through B.C.'s southern mountains, had a problem. How do you build a railway through a narrow, rock-walled canyon that is already filled wall-to-wall with a roaring river?

To survey the route, McCulloch was lowered by ropes from the top of the Coquihalla Canyon cliffs in a wicker basket. He decided to blast the railway line through the rock walls. His eventual route included four tunnels and crossed the river twice. Workers used cliff ladders, suspension bridges, and ropes to build it.

It was likely the world's most expensive section of railway track to build. Today the tracks are gone, but you can walk or bike on the old rail bed through the tunnels and alongside the thundering river. It's impressive!

Great ride, eh? We're right on track.

I think maybe I prefer flying.

Are they going to hibernate in there or what?

BUILDING A RAILWAY THROUGH (AND I MEAN THROUGH) THE ROCKY MOUNTAINS

What an uphill climb! The "big hill" in the Rocky Mountains was the steepest section of the whole CPR line. Four locomotives were needed to push freight cars up this hill.

There had to be an easier way through the mountains. How about … a spiral tunnel! That's what the engineers built in 1909. It allowed trains to gain elevation gradually as they zigzagged and circled through two mountains.

If you're driving the Trans-Canada Highway through Yoho National Park today, you can stop at the viewpoint to watch trains come through the spiral tunnel.

SLOW
ROAD AND CANAL
CONSTRUCTION
AHEAD

61

Building Highways and Waterways: Where There's a Will, There's a Way

How are we going to get ships across the land? Drive trucks over muskeg and mountains? Transport goods from one part of this humongous country to another? We'll build canals, then we'll bulldoze roads. We'll even build by hand if we have to. We'll face no end of big challenges, but we'll persevere. When the going gets tough, the tough get going! Well, don't just stand there—start building!

HOW DOES A FREIGHTER CLIMB STAIRS?

Not the way it shows in the picture. The stairs on the Welland Canal are actually called locks. Each lock has watertight steel gates at either end. When a freighter sails into the lock enclosure, the gates close. A valve then opens and water pours in from the canal upstream. The freighter floats higher and higher, until the water in the lock enclosure is at the same level as the water upstream. Then the upstream gate opens and the freighter sails out.

WELLAND CANAL

Canada has the largest water staircase in the world, the Welland Canal. It was first built in 1829, but it has been improved several times since then. Freighters climb fifteen-metre stairs to get from Lake Ontario up to Lake Erie, which is almost a hundred metres higher. If it weren't for the Welland Canal, freighters would have to sail up Niagara Falls! As you can imagine, that is not a recommended freighter route.

ST. LAWRENCE SEAWAY —DIG IT!

The Welland Canal is just one set of stairs in an even bigger construction project—the St. Lawrence Seaway. The project, which the United States and Canada worked on together for four years in the 1950s, allows inland-bound freighters to sail all the way from the Atlantic Ocean to the west shore of Lake Superior. At the time, it was the biggest man-made alteration to the earth's surface.

Workers dredged the bottom of the St. Lawrence River to make it deeper. They created canals and locks around rapids, and built power dams to provide electricity for the locks. There are now seven locks between Montreal and Lake Ontario, eight on the Welland Canal, and one last one at Sault Ste. Marie to boost ships up to Lake Superior.

RIDEAU CANAL

Let's say you wanted to travel from Montreal to Kingston (on Lake Ontario). The logical water route is up the St. Lawrence River. But after the War of 1812, the British were worried that the Americans might attack again and block the St. Lawrence. Then how would British troops and supplies get to Kingston, an important military base?

Time for Plan B. In 1826, the British started building the Rideau Canal—a sneaky alternative water route from Ottawa to Kingston. Lt. Col. John By was in charge. The 200-kilometre canal was built by hand over five years. It contains forty-seven locks to lift and lower ships through pools of different water levels (made by damming natural creeks and rivers). One of the dams built was the highest in North America at the time.

NO BUNGIE JUMPING FROM THIS BRIDGE

The Confederation Bridge linking New Brunswick and Prince Edward Island is almost thirteen kilometres long—long enough to need a curve in it to keep drivers awake. Built in 1997, it is designed to handle the worst winter conditions, not to mention earthquakes. Barriers (each one and a half metres high) along the sides of the bridge protect traffic from high winds. The base of the piers holding up the bridge have cone-shaped shields to deflect ice floes that push against them. At the bridge's highest point, it is sixty metres above the water.

Sixty metres ... that would be as high as thirty stacked moose!
I pity the moose at the bottom of the stack.
These are metaphorical moose.
They don't really exist.
Then what are they doing under Confederation Bridge?
I'm using them as a comparison to show you how high sixty metres would be.
Wouldn't they drown in the waters of the Northumberland Strait?
Goose, just forget the moose, okay?
Forget I mentioned them.
Those poor squished, drowned animals.

GO NORTH—AND HURRY UP ABOUT IT!

One of the biggest road-building projects in history, the Alaska Highway, was completed in a rush because of fear of enemy attack. At the beginning of the Second World War, the Americans were worried that the Japanese might attack the West Coast of Canada or Alaska. No road or railway existed to get troops and supplies to Alaska to repel this attack if it happened.

So in 1942, the United States Army started bulldozing a 2,451-kilometre supply road from Dawson Creek, B.C. (the end of the existing rail line), to Fairbanks, Alaska. Around mountains, over muskeg, through forests, and over rivers. Rush, rush.

It was no easy task. Heavy equipment was swallowed up by muskeg. Bridges were washed out. Thousands of Americans and Canadians worked seven long days a week for eight and a half months to get the road finished. (After all that, the Japanese never showed.)

The Alaska Highway has been vastly improved since then. Today you can cruise in the comfort of your RV from British Columbia to the Yukon or Alaska.

Canada's Trans-Canada Highway is more than 7,000 kilometres long—making it the longest national highway in the world!
Are we there yet?
Work out the math, Goose. If we drive at an average speed of a hundred kilometres an hour, and we travel for ten hours a day without stopping, we can get across Canada in a week.
How will we get back?
We'll fly!

Big Dams, Mines, and Pipelines

People think BIG in Canada—it's that kind of a country. Massive dams for hydroelectric power, huge mines, pipelines stretching from one side of the country to the other—Canadians have made them all. Get ready for big stuff!

BIG DAMS

We've got power in our fast-flowing rivers, so we've built some whopper hydroelectric dams to tap into this energy source. Falling water turns a water wheel (called a turbine), which then turns a generator, which creates electric power.

The James Bay Project in northern Quebec is the grand-daddy of all hydroelectric-generating projects. Eight dams were built, one with a spillway (where the surplus water spills over the dam and falls to the river below) three times the height of Niagara Falls. Smaller rivers were diverted to increase the flow of the main river, called La Grande Rivière, and huge areas of wilderness were flooded.

BIG MINES

There's buried treasure in Canada, but to find it, you have to dig!

The open-pit copper mine at Logan Lake, B.C.—Canada's largest mine—is so big it can be seen from the moon. The pit, shaped like a gigantic bowl, is two kilometres across. The over-sized diggers and trucks working in the pit look like tiny toys in comparison.

The deepest underground mine shaft in Canada is at the Macassa gold mine in Kirkland Lake, Ontario. It goes down more than two kilometres! (A mine in Timmins, Ontario, now closed, went even deeper—two and a half kilometres. It was the world's deepest mine.)

BIG PIPELINES

Mammoth Canadian pipelines snake across the land carrying oil and natural gas from wells (often in Alberta) to customers (usually in eastern Canada). The world's longest petroleum pipeline carries crude oil from Alberta to Sarnia, Ontario. Electric motors propel the oil at about walking speed along the 11,500 kilometres of steel pipe. The trip takes a month.

Pipelines are buried under a metre or more of earth and snow. Engineers have invented huge trenching machines to dig ditches for the pipes. Remote-controlled robots, called pigs, move along the inside of the pipes to clean them and detect any damage.

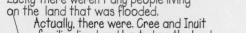

Lucky there weren't any people living on the land that was flooded.

Actually, there were. Cree and Inuit families lived and hunted on the land. They weren't happy to find out that rivers would be dammed and land flooded to provide electricity for people living in cities to the south. Eventually, they signed an agreement with the government that allowed construction to go ahead but gave them payment and other benefits in return.

BUILDING A BIG BOONDOGGLE: THE CANOL PIPELINE

During the Second World War, the Americans wanted a good supply of oil to use to fuel any defence of Alaska against a possible Japanese attack. They thought oil tankers travelling along the coast would be vulnerable, so they couldn't send oil that way.

That's why the U.S. army built the Canol (short for "Canadian oil") Pipeline— an oil pipeline that ran through almost a thousand kilometres of northern wilderness. It went from oilfields in the Mackenzie River valley, at Norman Wells, to Whitehorse, site of an oil refinery. It was an incredibly expensive project, and everything seemed to go wrong. Many times, the pipeline was damaged by washouts and slides. The oil flowed for only one year before the U.S. government decided it would be a lot cheaper to send it by ship.

Today the abandoned pipeline route, known as the Canol Trail, is used by hikers.

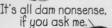

It's all dam nonsense, if you ask me.

I didn't ask you.

DIGGING FOR DIAMONDS

Canada's first diamond mine was in the Northwest Territories, 300 kilometres northeast of Yellowknife. Because it's so remote, it's a very inconvenient place for a mine.

To get the initial building supplies to the mine site, the company built a 440-kilometre winter road. But it is frozen hard enough to use for only ten weeks of the year. (The rest of the time it is mushy and wet.) The 2,000 truckloads of equipment and supplies needed to construct the mine all had to be transported to the mine site during one ten-week period. The company eventually built an open-pit mine, a processing plant surrounded by an insulated skin to keep out the cold, an airstrip, and a 375-room hotel. It was the largest building project ever undertaken north of Canada's treeline.

Amazing what some folks will do for diamonds!

HARD HAT ZONE

Made in Canada!

From coast to coast to coast, Canadians have built many other things that are fascinating, impressive, or downright weird. Unfortunately, we can show only a sampling here. But look around where you live, and you're sure to find more.

WEST EDMONTON MALL

Attention, shoppers! This is the world's largest shopping mall. It's so huge that it's like a complete city under one roof. You can visit 800 stores, play in the world's largest water park, ice-skate, play minigolf, take a submarine ride through a pretend ocean, scuba dive, or lose your breakfast during the Drop of Doom ride in Fantasyland. The West Ed Mall is so big that you can even rent little motorized scooters to help you get around.

Can you tell me where the exit is?

Exit? No idea. I haven't been out for years!

ALPHABETICAL RAILWAY TOWNS

Look carefully at the names of towns on the Prairies and you might notice something really interesting. There are strings of towns whose names are in alphabetical order. One alphabetical string starts with Arona (in Manitoba) and goes to Zeneta (in Saskatchewan). Another begins with Atwater and goes to Zelma (both in Saskatchewan). These places were once stations on the railways that crossed the Prairies. Many stations have since disappeared, however, leaving gaps in the alphabet.

Did someone actually weigh 23,200 elephants?

DON'T LOOK DOWN!

The CN Tower in Toronto is bigger than the Eiffel Tower in Paris and New York's Empire State Building. It is 533 metres high, and it weighs more than 23,200 elephants. You can ride a glass elevator up to a lookout near the top. Once there, you can step onto a glass floor and look down to the ground beneath your feet—113 storeys down! If you dare.

ALLAN   BRADWELL   CLAVET   DURO   EATON

MEGALOPOLIS

Try standing at a busy street corner in Toronto, being careful not to get run over by streetcars or pedestrians. Imagine you're alone in a cool, quiet forest. Hard, isn't it? Yet once this area *was* covered in forest.

Not any more! The area shown in this satellite photo is just a tiny part of Canada at the western end of Lake Ontario. Yet this is now home to one-fifth of Canada's population. People have built houses, apartment buildings, skyscrapers, department stores, factories, roads, highways, highways passing over other highways, and plenty of parking lots.

One more interesting fact—this area has Canada's most fertile farmland. Hmm. Do you see a problem here?

GREEN GABLES INC.

Visitors by the busload come to see a pretty white house with green shutters on Prince Edward Island. It's the setting for Lucy Maud Montgomery's famous book *Anne of Green Gables*. Fans from around the world want to see where Anne lived (even though she's an imaginary character who never really lived there). Many tourists come from Japan, where *Anne of Green Gables* (translated as *Anne of the Red Hair*) is an enormous bestseller. Green Gables now has a museum and a gift shop attached.

I'm going to write another sequel: Anne of the Gift Shoppe.

THE BIG O

What a great idea! Build a roof that can be open or closed, depending on the weather. That's what designers had in mind for the Olympic Stadium in Montreal, where the Montreal Expos play baseball. The stadium is fondly known as the Big O. The Big *Uh-Oh* is more like it! The roof never worked properly, and once it even partially collapsed, sending tons of concrete crashing down. Now it stays shut permanently.

Ooops! I'm out of order.

EXCEEDINGLY WEIRD

A sea-going ship in Saskatchewan? A strange tourist attraction is an ocean-going vessel built on the Prairies in the early 1900s. Ted Sukanen's ship sits near Moose Jaw, far from the sea. His plan was to sail it to Finland by way of the South Saskatchewan River and Hudson Bay. He died before he could finish the work.

FARLEY   MOOSE   HAWOODS   KINLEY

STORM WARNING

Chapter 5

Weather Weirdness

Pull on your rain boots, your snow mitts, and your sun hat! The forecast for this chapter is extreme weather with occasional flooding and a 90 per cent chance of bizarre things falling from the sky.

Honk-ing in the rain!
Honk-ing in the rain!

Forecast: increasing silliness.

Incredible weather weirdness

More true tales of wild weather

Things falling from the sky

Hang on to your hat!

Wacky weather awards

Well, look who just blew in!

It's windy out there. I wasn't sure I was going to be able to land in this weather.

It's getting wild, isn't it? The barometer is falling.

Quick! Catch it.

Catch what?

The barometer.

No, Goose. A barometer is an instrument that measures air pressure. When I say the barometer is falling, I mean the air pressure is getting lower. Falling air pressure usually means bad weather is moving in.

Who needs barometers? When my tail feathers blow inside out, I know it's lousy weather. That wind blew like it was a hurry-cane!

You mean a hurricane? Obviously we should talk about weather, Goose. Canadians are always talking about the weather.

There's always lots of weather to talk about.

To heck with talking—we should do something about it!

What are you going to do about Canadian weather?

Weather forecasters should take action instead of just waiting for weather to happen. Slow down the hurry-canes! Sew up the torn-adoes! And when it starts to rain, start honking!

Honking in the rain?

Sure. Haven't you heard that song?

Can You Believe This Weather?

True stories, incredible incidents, and outlandish happenings?
Blame it on the weather!

THE GREAT ESCAPE

On August 24, 1998, a huge balloon twenty-five storeys high was launched from a field in Saskatchewan. Made of ultra-thin plastic and inflated with enough helium to fill Toronto's SkyDome, the balloon rose thirty-eight kilometres above the earth into the ozone layer. Dangling from a cable attached to the balloon were expensive meteorological instruments that would collect information about the ozone layer for a period of twenty-four hours.

When the twenty-four hours were up, according to the plan, small remote-controlled explosions would cut the cable that attached the instruments to the balloon. The instruments would parachute down to earth. At the same time, a flap would rip open on top of the balloon so it would deflate and descend to a soft landing in Alberta.

That's not what happened. The flap did open, but the immense, now partially deflated balloon drifted off on a voyage across the North Atlantic. The chase was on! The Canadian military sent out two CF-18 fighter jets and blasted the balloon with a thousand rounds of twenty-millimetre cannon shells, but even that didn't do the job. Commercial airlines were rerouted to avoid a collision. The balloon travelled over the Arctic Ocean, headed towards Russia, then looped back to Finland. Finally, ten days after it had escaped, the runaway balloon touched down in a Finnish farmer's field.

70

FRIED EGGS ON THE SIDEWALK

Want your egg cooked sunny side up? During Canada's worst heat wave, in July 1936, you could fry eggs on the sidewalk! Manitoba's highest recorded temperature was 44.4°C. (A pleasant summertime temperature is about 28°C.) Saskatchewan and Ontario were almost as hot. Steel rail lines twisted in the heat, crops dried up, and fruit baked on the trees. Sales of ice cream and soft drinks in Toronto went up 50 per cent!

AMAZING SIGHTS: THE NORTHERN LIGHTS

Stay up late and watch the fireworks! Nature's own fireworks display is most commonly seen on winter nights in the North. The northern lights (also called the aurora borealis) produce curtains of colour that shimmer, dance, and swirl across the sky. They are caused when solar winds (electrically charged particles from the sun travelling at supersonic speeds) collide with atoms and molecules in the earth's atmosphere. Different atmospheric gases radiate different colours of light.

This awesome solar-powered light show can sometimes create bizarre special effects here on earth, triggering burglar alarms, opening automatic garage doors, interfering with TV reception, and causing electrical blowouts. On March 13, 1989, a particularly spectacular display of the northern lights—which could be seen as far south as Jamaica—caused an energy surge that cut power to the entire province of Quebec!

INCREDIBLE FROZEN TODDLERS

Extreme cold can kill. It's amazing that it didn't kill two small tykes from the Prairies.

A two-year-old from Rouleau, Saskatchewan, wandered out of her house on a frigid February night in 1994 and was accidentally locked out. The wind chill (low temperatures combined with wind) froze her flesh within thirty seconds. When she was found six hours later, she looked dead. Her body temperature was 14°C (a normal body temperature is about 37°C). Incredibly, medical staff were able to warm the small child's blood and bring her back to life, although she did lose one leg below the knee to frostbite. (When people survive extreme cold, it's because their metabolism slows down at low temperatures and their oxygen and energy requirements drop. Children are more likely to survive because their small bodies cool much more quickly, which offers a better chance of survival and limited permanent physical damage.)

A similarly miraculous story took place in February 2001, when a thirteen-month-old toddler left her bed and wandered outside into bone-numbing temperatures. When her frantic mother finally found her, her body temperature was down to 15°C. But doctors slowly warmed her up, and her heart started beating again. Her astounding recovery made news around the world!

Forecast: Freezing Rain, Floods, Drought ... and Groundhogs?

More True Tales (Really. Honestly.)

There are so many exciting ways to get wet, cold, and miserable in Canada. Our weather provides no end of character-building experiences, and we always have something to talk about. Let's check it out! (If you really want to have fun, bring your football.)

HOGGING THE WEATHER FORECAST

Wiarton Willie is the most famous weather-forecasting groundhog in Canada. Every year on Groundhog Day, reporters flock to Wiarton, Ontario, to watch as Willie emerges from hibernation to predict the coming of spring. The albino groundhog even has his own Web site.

You've heard about Groundhog Day, of course. Here's how the legend goes: On February 2 of each year, at precisely noon, a groundhog comes out of its underground burrow. If it's a sunny day, the groundhog sees its shadow. Startled, it hops back into its hole to sleep for six more weeks of winter. If it's not a sunny day, the groundhog doesn't see its shadow and isn't frightened back into its hole. The groundhog stays out, and this is supposed to mean that the worst of winter is over and warmer weather is on its way.

Tragedy struck Wiarton Willie in 1999. When Willie's handler went to rouse him to give his annual forecast, his burrow was silent. Willie was dead, and thousands mourned his passing. But life goes on, and fortunately Wee Willie Jr., also a white groundhog, has taken over the job and continues to provide the annual Groundhog Day prediction.

How accurate is a weather forecast from a groundhog? According to the weather experts, not very.

Yup, there's definitely weather out here.

Wiarton Willie the First

Not very accurate? How accurate are the official forecasts? I bet groundhogs do just as well as the experts!

ATTACK OF THE KILLER ICE

The ice storm of the century struck eastern Canada and the United States in January 1998. Rain fell from a layer of warm air trapped above a much colder layer. It froze when it hit the ground, coating everything with a thick sheet of ice. Trees collapsed under loads thirty times their own weight. Transmission towers crumpled. Twenty-five people in Ontario and Quebec died. More than a million Canadians spent several days without power, shivering in the cold and darkness.

WANTED: RAIN!

During the Dustbowl Era, from 1933 to 1937, the Canadian Prairies received only 60 per cent of their normal rainfall. Dry soil turned to dust and blew away. Crops dried up and animals starved. A quarter of a million people were forced to abandon their land.

FUMBLING FOOTBALLS

The Canadian Football League's Grey Cup game is always played in November. The weather is frequently unfriendly, as you can see from these soggy, foggy examples below.

The 1939 Snow Bowl: During this game in Ottawa, swirling snow made visibility so bad that fans were asked to park their cars along the sidelines of the field and turn their headlights on.

The 1950 Mud Bowl: The day before this Toronto game there was a record twenty-five-centimetre snowfall. On Grey Cup day, melting snow combined with rain to make the field look like a mud-wrestling arena. When players were tackled, they slid in the mud. One quarterback secretly taped thumbtacks to his fingers so he could hang on to the slippery ball.

The 1952 Fog Bowl: It was so foggy in Toronto two years later that spectators in the upper stands couldn't see what was happening on the field. When conditions got even worse, the game had to be stopped and rescheduled for the following day.

The 1965 Wind Bowl: When players punted the ball during this game in Toronto, the wind, gusting to eighty kilometres an hour, actually blew it backwards.

Those were exciting days in Canadian football. Now that many cities have covered stadiums, football just isn't as much fun!

Precipitation Alert: Don't Turn This Page! (Don't Say I Didn't Warn You)

Don't Look Up!

Take cover! The sky isn't falling, but almost everything else is.
Rain, hail, snow—even fish!

AVALANCHE ALERT

Avalanches are always a danger in the mountains. Snow piles up on the steep slopes, and when it gets heavy enough, it starts to slide. In a big avalanche, thousands of tons of snow can thunder down a mountain at speeds of up to 300 kilometres an hour. You don't want to be there when that happens!

BURIED IN SNOW

Canada's worst avalanche happened on March 5, 1910, at Rogers Pass, in British Columbia, where the Canadian Pacific Railway wound through the steep slopes of the Selkirk Mountains. First, a slide came down one side of the narrow valley, burying a section of track. While railway workers were removing this snow, a second avalanche tumbled down from the slopes on the other side of the valley, burying sixty-two of the workers under ten metres of snow.

That was only the worst of many fatal snow slides that occurred along this stretch of track. Between 1885 and 1911, 200 railway workers were killed here by avalanches. Eventually, the railway operators gave up the snow war and rerouted the line through tunnels underneath the mountains.

But today the Trans-Canada Highway winds through Rogers Pass and avalanches are still a problem. Sometimes the highway threads through snow sheds that have been constructed to allow snow to slide right over top of the road—not across the road surface. When there is a dangerous build-up of snow on the slopes, avalanche technicians start avalanches on purpose! First, of course, the highway is closed. Then the technicians fire explosives at the slopes from artillery guns. This shakes the snow and starts it sliding. Once the avalanches have come down safely, the highway crew cleans up the road and the highway is reopened—until the next snow build-up occurs.

THIS SNOW'S NO GOOD

Canada is known as the land of ice and snow, but this is ridiculous! During a phenomenal snowstorm in Montreal in March 1971, 110-kilometre winds piled snowdrifts so high they reached second-storey windows! It took two weeks to get the streets open. Trucks had to haul away 500,000 loads of snow.

A huge blizzard hit the southern Prairies in the winter of 1947, burying towns and railways from Calgary to Winnipeg. Snowdrifts in that storm were so high that people had to build tunnels to get to their outhouses! One Saskatchewan farmer headed out to the barn to milk his cows, but he couldn't get in through the door because it was blocked by snow. He had to cut a hole in the barn roof and climb through!

THE BIG SPLOOSH!

Rain began to fall in the Saguenay River region of Quebec on July 19, 1996. (The Saguenay River flows into the St. Lawrence.) It rained, it poured, and it didn't stop. Swollen creeks filled reservoirs until they overflowed. Dikes and dams burst. Torrents of water carrying boulders, mud, and trees carved out new river channels. The floods washed away bridges, roads, and houses in cities like Chicoutimi, Jonquière, and La Baie. The Saguenay floods were the worst in Canada's history.

Good weather for ducks—but not much else!

One time, it rained cooked geese! In 1932, a lightning bolt hit a flock of geese flying over Elgin, Ontario, and fried them. People found the geese on the ground and ate them for supper.
I don't think that's funny.
I guess you wouldn't.

How about this for weirdness? It once rained fish on Toronto! A school of flying fish—the kind that leap into the air—got caught by a freak wind while they were airborne and were blown over the city before falling to the ground. Sounds very fishy, but is it any weirder than when it rains cats and dogs?

VERY HIGH WINDS

Gale warning! Tornado forecast! Hurricane alert! Hang on to your hat ...

Amazing Tornado! It just blew me away!

TORNADO TALES

Canada gets many tornadoes. Fortunately, only a few are real humdingers!

When the Regina Cyclone swept through Regina, Saskatchewan, on June 30, 1912, it scattered year-end school examination papers. Teachers had to pass or fail students without knowing their exam marks. (I'll bet you sometimes wish a tornado would blow away your schoolwork!) That was the least of the damage caused by this tornado, however. It lasted only three minutes but left at least twenty-eight people dead, hundreds injured, and a quarter of the population of the city homeless. It was rated force 4, which means the winds were between 330 and 416 kilometres an hour. It was the worst tornado in Canadian history.

Some other tornadoes have caused strange things to happen. On July 12, 1947, for instance, a man and his four-year-old son were sleeping when one slammed into their home on Walpole Island, on Lake St. Clair, Ontario. The tornado lifted the house and dropped it back upside down. The mattress on which the man and his son were sleeping landed on top of them, and the remainder of the house on top of that. Luckily, they both survived.

Another tornado blew across southern Ontario on May 23, 1953. When a crew from an appliance store later arrived to install a new gas stove at a home near Woodstock, in the tornado area, the house had vanished!

ABOUT TORNADOES: TWIST AND SHOUT ROAR

A violent tornado, or twister, can leave a narrow path of destruction across the land. Tornadoes form within the unstable air of a thunderhead (a kind of cloud that usually means a thunderstorm is coming). When a swirling funnel of air drops down from the cloud towards the ground, you have a tornado. Tornadoes are rated from force 0 to force 5, depending on their strength. Most twisters in Canada are force 0 or force 1, but we have had some force 4s. They are most common in the southern Prairies and southwestern Ontario, which are the regions most prone to the unstable air masses tornadoes come from.

There are many stories about the strange things tornadoes do, such as destroying one house but sparing the house next door, moving henhouses without cracking the eggs, or lifting babies and setting them down unharmed.

The Black Friday Tornado hit Edmonton on July 31, 1987, killing twenty-seven people. Winds reached 400 kilometres an hour, and hail as large as softballs fell on the city.

PSST! WANNA KNOW THE HURRICANE FORECAST?

Back in 1873, before hurricanes were given names, a monster one smashed into Cape Breton Island in Nova Scotia. A thousand people died and 1,200 ships were lost. Weather forecasters in Toronto knew a day in advance that the hurricane was coming, but people living in Cape Breton Island had no warning. The telegraph lines to Halifax weren't working, so the Toronto forecasters couldn't send an alert. That disaster prompted the government to develop a national weather-warning system. Once it was in place, forecasters could send weather information across the country in an instant. Today anyone can find up-to-date weather information on the Internet.

HURRIBLE HORRICANES

Canada doesn't get many hurricanes. They form in the tropics, near the equator, and by the time such storms spiral north to Canada, they're usually not in a hurry. But there have been exceptions.

Hurricane Hazel went on a rampage through Toronto and southern Ontario in 1954. With torrential rain causing flash floods, some residents had to climb onto their roofs and grab hold of television antennae to escape the fast-rising water. Streets, bridges, houses, trees, and bodies were swept away.

Typhoon Freda ("typhoon" is another name for a hurricane) blasted British Columbia's west coast in 1962 with winds gusting up to 145 kilometres an hour. In 1971, Hurricane Beth deluged Nova Scotia with almost three metres of rain.

WHAT A BLAST

Holy hair dryer! Imagine a blast of warm wind that suddenly sends temperatures soaring from –19°C to 22°C in one hour. It happened in Pincher Creek, Alberta, in January 1962. Welcome to chinook country!

Chinooks are warm, gusty winds that howl across southwestern Alberta. They form when warm, moist air from the Pacific Ocean blows inland, lifting over British Columbia's mountains. As the air rises, the water vapour in it condenses into rain or snow that falls on the western mountain slopes. Now the wind is dry, and when it plunges down the eastern slopes of the Rocky Mountains and onto the Prairies, it cranks up the heat and gobbles up the snow.

77

Where It's Hot and Where It's Not

Meet the wettest, hottest, snowiest, windiest, hailstone-iest places in Canada! The competition was fierce for the top spots, but the winners are ... (Pass the envelope, please.)

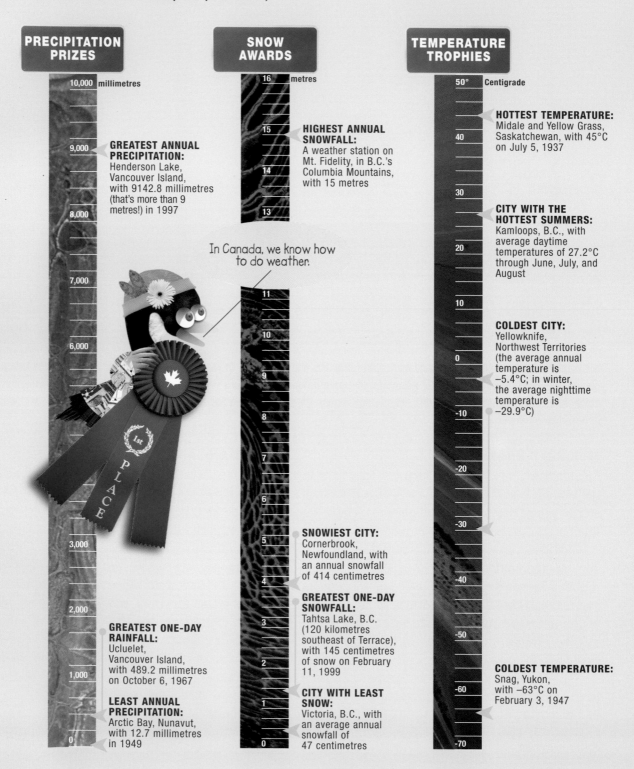

PRECIPITATION PRIZES

10,000 millimetres

GREATEST ANNUAL PRECIPITATION:
Henderson Lake, Vancouver Island, with 9142.8 millimetres (that's more than 9 metres!) in 1997

GREATEST ONE-DAY RAINFALL:
Ucluelet, Vancouver Island, with 489.2 millimetres on October 6, 1967

LEAST ANNUAL PRECIPITATION:
Arctic Bay, Nunavut, with 12.7 millimetres in 1949

SNOW AWARDS

16 metres

HIGHEST ANNUAL SNOWFALL:
A weather station on Mt. Fidelity, in B.C.'s Columbia Mountains, with 15 metres

In Canada, we know how to do weather.

SNOWIEST CITY:
Cornerbrook, Newfoundland, with an annual snowfall of 414 centimetres

GREATEST ONE-DAY SNOWFALL:
Tahtsa Lake, B.C. (120 kilometres southeast of Terrace), with 145 centimetres of snow on February 11, 1999

CITY WITH LEAST SNOW:
Victoria, B.C., with an average annual snowfall of 47 centimetres

TEMPERATURE TROPHIES

50° Centigrade

HOTTEST TEMPERATURE:
Midale and Yellow Grass, Saskatchewan, with 45°C on July 5, 1937

CITY WITH THE HOTTEST SUMMERS:
Kamloops, B.C., with average daytime temperatures of 27.2°C through June, July, and August

COLDEST CITY:
Yellowknife, Northwest Territories (the average annual temperature is −5.4°C; in winter, the average nighttime temperature is −29.9°C)

COLDEST TEMPERATURE:
Snag, Yukon, with −63°C on February 3, 1947

MOST SUMMER SUNSHINE:
Yellowknife,
Northwest Territories

WINDIEST SPOT:
Cape Warwick,
on Resolution Island,
Nunavut, with an
average annual wind
speed of thirty-six
kilometres an hour

Fowl weather, eh?

FOGGIEST CITY:
St. John's, Newfoundland

Cape Warwick

WINDIEST CITY:
St. John's, Newfoundland,
with an average annual
wind speed of twenty-four
kilometres an hour

Yellowknife

St. John's

LOUDIEST CITY:
Prince Rupert, B.C.

Prince Rupert

Cedoux

Winnipeg

Ottawa

HIGHEST HUMIDITY:
Windsor, Ontario

Windsor

During a record-breaking hailstorm
in Cedoux, Saskatchewan, a hailstone
weighed in at 290 grams (as much as
a can of soup).

Canadians can be proud of Ottawa.
Because it's our national capital!
Not just that. Ottawa is the coldest
national capital in the world, with
the exception of ... um, Ulaanbaatar,
Mongolia.
I'm so darn proud,
I've got goosebumps!

Chill out, dudes.
Yellowknife is
Canada's coldest
city!

Ottawa is cold, but
Winnipeg is colder!
But it's a dry cold.

**Caution:
Kooky Canucks**

79

Chapter 6

So You Think Canadians Are Boring? Ha!

Take off to adventure! You won't meet Martians, but the Canadians in this chapter are definitely different. They're outstanding, outlandish, and in some cases, out to lunch! They think outside the box. Canadians boring? Not a chance!

Folks who rob trains, assume fake identities, and shoot would-be assassins

Canadians who are famous! Infamous! Definitely hard to ignore

Go-getters who migrate with geese or go looking for bear trouble

Inventors of incredible stuff (Why didn't I think of that?)

Gigantic roadside attractions—from lobsters to geese

Do you have a box I could use?
How big a box?
I dunno. I just want one so
I can "think outside the box."
In that case, a small box
will do fine.
Maybe even a box of cookies?

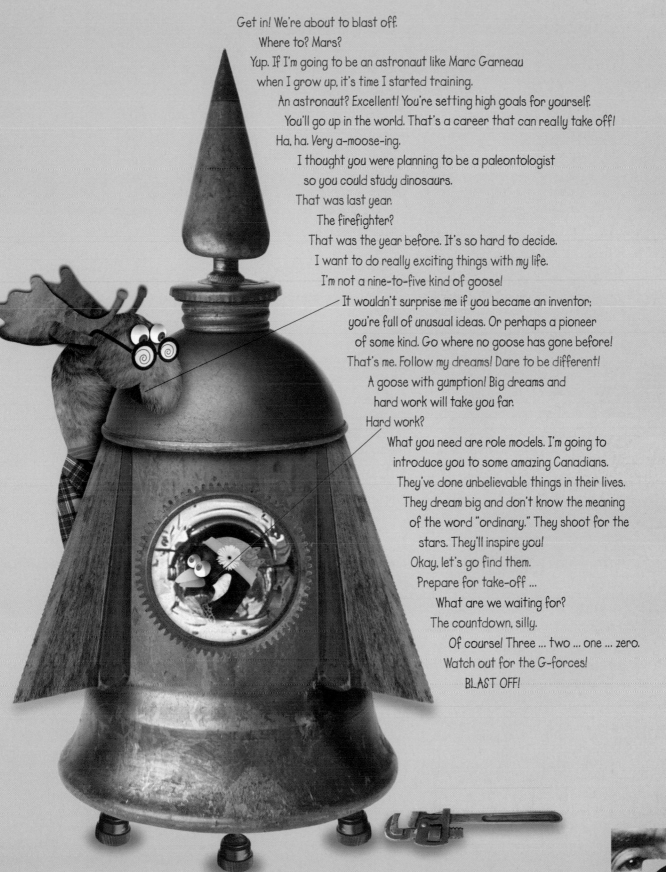

Get in! We're about to blast off.

Where to? Mars?

Yup. If I'm going to be an astronaut like Marc Garneau
when I grow up, it's time I started training.

An astronaut? Excellent! You're setting high goals for yourself.
You'll go up in the world. That's a career that can really take off!

Ha, ha. Very a-moose-ing.

I thought you were planning to be a paleontologist
so you could study dinosaurs.

That was last year.

The firefighter?

That was the year before. It's so hard to decide.
I want to do really exciting things with my life.
I'm not a nine-to-five kind of goose!

It wouldn't surprise me if you became an inventor;
you're full of unusual ideas. Or perhaps a pioneer
of some kind. Go where no goose has gone before!

That's me. Follow my dreams! Dare to be different!

A goose with gumption! Big dreams and
hard work will take you far.

Hard work?

What you need are role models. I'm going to
introduce you to some amazing Canadians.
They've done unbelievable things in their lives.
They dream big and don't know the meaning
of the word "ordinary." They shoot for the
stars. They'll inspire you!

Okay, let's go find them.

Prepare for take-off ...

What are we waiting for?

The countdown, silly.

Of course! Three ... two ... one ... zero.

Watch out for the G-forces!

BLAST OFF!

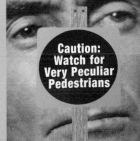

Caution:
Watch for
Very Peculiar
Pedestrians

Unusual, Unconventional, Unbelievably Unboring Canadians

You want respectable, well-behaved, ordinary Canadians? Go somewhere else! The individuals you'll meet here are ... um, different.

Will James

So the cowboy everybody thought was Will James was actually Ernest Dufault?

That's right. Where there's a Will, there's an Ernest!

Moose, you're weird.

COWBOYS ...

Ride 'em cowboy! Meet Will James, the legendary cowboy of the American Wild West. In the early 1900s, every little kid dreamed of being a real cowboy like Will James. Not only could he rope a steer, but he also wrote and illustrated twenty-four books about life in the saddle.

According to James, he was born in Montana on a wagon train. His mother died when he was a year old, and three years later, his father was speared to death by the horn of a steer in a corral during a roundup. James was then brought up by a French-Canadian trapper who died when the boy was just thirteen. (That, he insisted, explained his French accent.)

Great story, but none of it was true.

Will James was actually a French Canadian named Ernest Dufault who was born in St-Nazaire d'Acton, Quebec, in 1892. He hardly spoke a word of English until he was in his teens. At fifteen, he took the train west to the Canadian Prairies, where he began his cowboy career. Eventually, he transformed himself into Will James and moved to the United States. On a visit home to Quebec, he collected and destroyed every photograph or bit of evidence of his real childhood.

The truth about Will James's identity was uncovered twenty-five years after his death. An author writing a biography of the famous cowboy stumbled upon his will and discovered that it left part of his estate to a relative named "Default" in Ontario.

AND INDIANS

Grey Owl, dressed in his feathers, beads, and buckskin, was a truly inspiring sight. People were fascinated by his tales of life in northern Saskatchewan. They especially loved hearing about his two pet beavers, Rawhide and Jelly Roll. When Grey Owl went on speaking tours in England, he was a huge attraction. He was even invited to meet the king!

According to Grey Owl, his father was Scottish and his mother Apache. He spent his boyhood years working as a knife thrower in Buffalo Bill's Wild West Show.

But after Grey Owl died, it was discovered that he wasn't Native at all! He was actually an Englishman named Archibald Stansfield Belaney. As an unhappy boy, Belaney had been fascinated by North American Indians. He even dreamed of becoming one—so he did!

Grey Owl

OUTFOXED!

Train robberies were Billy Miner's specialty. He was a career criminal who started robbing stagecoaches in the American West when he was just sixteen. Between hold-ups, he spent a lot of time in prison. Released from jail in 1904, when he was almost sixty years old, Miner came north to Canada, settled in the British Columbia interior, and presented himself as a respectable gentleman rancher. Don't believe it! The Grey Fox, as he was called, and his gang held up two Canadian Pacific Railway trains, the first in 1904 and the second in 1906. After a huge manhunt, the outlaw was captured.

The Grey Fox was sentenced to life and held in a prison near Vancouver. The railway wasn't entirely happy, however. You see, Miner had buried $300,000 of stolen government bonds somewhere. Unless the CPR got them back, the company knew it would have to reimburse the government for that lost money.

CPR detectives visited Miner in 1908 and quietly promised to get him set free if he would tell them where the money was buried. Within three months, Miner had "escaped" from prison and the CPR had delivered the bonds to the government. There was an uproar in the Canadian Parliament, but the Grey Fox had already fled south across the border. He was on his way to rob another train in Georgia (where he was arrested in 1911). He died in 1913 in prison.

TWO-GUN COHEN

What a life! At sixteen, in about 1905, Morris Cohen was sent from his home in London, England, to Saskatchewan. There he learned to gamble and shoot. After saving the owner of a Chinese restaurant from a robbery, Cohen became interested in Chinese culture. He later became the personal bodyguard to a Chinese leader who was visiting Canada. Dr. Sun Yat-sen certainly needed one: there was a million-dollar bounty on his head. Many Chinese wanted to kill him because he was trying to overthrow their emperor.

In 1922, Cohen moved to China to become Dr. Sun Yat-sen's permanent bodyguard. China was at that time a closed, unknown country to most Canadians. But Cohen was in the middle of the action! He had many adventures and perilous close calls while protecting Sun Yat-sen from attempts on his life. After one battle in which Cohen got shot in the right arm, he decided he should learn to shoot with both hands. From then on, he packed two forty-five-calibre automatic pistols—and was known as Two-Gun Cohen.

Don't mess with me! I'm Two-Gun Goose!

I think you're taking this a little too far, Goose.

Big Shots Just Over the Page

Some Canadians Who've Made It BIG!

I really look up to Angus.

Angus McAskill

Average-Sized Man

ANNA SWAN starred in the Greatest Show on Earth, a famous circus in New York. You couldn't miss her! She was billed as being 246 centimetres tall, which was an exaggeration. She was actually only 228 centimetres. Tall enough!

When Anna was born, in Nova Scotia in 1846, she weighed eight kilograms. (Ask your parents what you weighed at birth—probably a puny three or four kilograms.) By the time she was twenty-two, Swan weighed 160 kilograms. She married an American who was even bigger than she was.

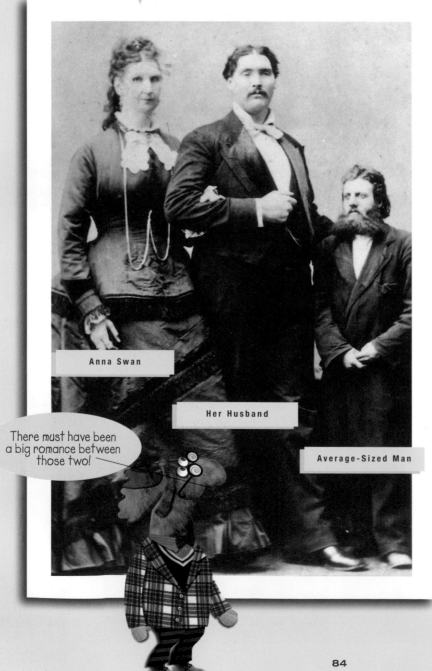

Anna Swan

Her Husband

Average-Sized Man

There must have been a big romance between those two!

ANGUS MCASKILL, you're one tall dude! The Cape Breton giant, born in 1825, was 236 centimetres tall and weighed 193 kilograms! While most exceptionally tall people have some disease that causes them to grow so big, McAskill was just naturally that way. He could lift huge loads, and his palms were the size of a page in this book.

THE GREAT ANTONIO lives in Montreal and claims to be the world's strongest man. He weighs 232 kilograms. His specialty is pulling loaded buses.

EMILY CARR is now famous for her bold paintings of the West Coast. Before she became well known, however, her neighbours in Victoria called her "Crazy Old Millie" Carr. She liked to wheel a pet monkey called Woo around in a baby carriage.

Mother?

NORMAN BETHUNE

Canada's Norman Bethune is a hero—in China! Bethune was born in 1890 in Gravenhurst, Ontario. He was a surgeon, an inventor, and a strong supporter of causes he believed in. He became a Communist and went to China to help battle against Japanese invaders in 1938. He treated wounded soldiers and trained thousands of Chinese as medics and doctors. Tragically, he died of blood poisoning after cutting himself during an operation.

To the Chinese and their leader, Mao Tse-tung, Bethune was a symbol of devotion to others. There's a statue of him in China, and a medical school and hospital were built in his name.

China was a closed and secret country for many years. When Canadians were finally allowed to visit, the Chinese gave them a particularly warm welcome—all because of a Canadian man called Norman Bethune.

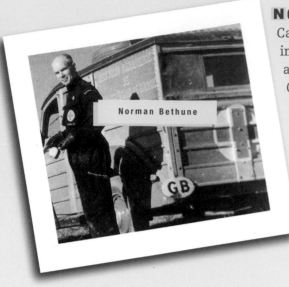

Norman Bethune

CAN YOU SEE ... QUINTUPLE?

They were a Canadian sensation! Annette, Emilie, Yvonne, Cécile, and Marie Dionne were quintuplets born in Corbeil, Ontario, on May 28, 1934. Identical quintuplets are incredibly rare, and never in recorded history had any lived more than a few weeks.

The government took the girls away from their parents and built a special hospital for their care. The Dionne Quints then made the government a lot of money by becoming Canada's biggest tourist attraction! The hospital had a playground with a public observation gallery, and 3 million people travelled to Quintland, as it came to be called, to watch the babies at play behind a one-way screen.

Later in life, after the deaths of Emilie and Marie, the remaining quintuplets sued the government for compensation for the way they were treated as children.

I'm unique!   Just like me!   And me!   Me too!   Ditto!

Dionne Quintuplets

What are you geese up to?
We're finding out what it would be like to be a tourist attraction.

Wurld-Famuss
Canada Goose Kwintuplets
Incredibul Turist Attrackshun!
Admishin Only $1!

Now, just look cute and don't hiss!

Less-Travelled Road Ahead— Expect the Unexpected

The Mind-Boggling Things Canadians Do

What are these Canadians doing? You may well ask! Falling off cliffs, migrating with birds, shooting down enemy planes, crossing Niagara Falls on tightropes ... well, at least they are keeping out of trouble.

IT'S A BIRD! IT'S A PLANE! AND IT'S BILL LISHMAN!

My hero!

Bill Lishman

Bill Lishman, from Blackstock, Ontario, just outside Toronto, pretends to be a bird. He teaches other birds to safely migrate south. But because he's actually a human, Lishman uses an ultralight plane to get airborne.

Birds normally imprint on (or attach to) the first things they see when they hatch out of their eggs. Lishman wants the baby birds to imprint on his airplane. While still in their eggs, the birds are played recordings of airplane engine noise. When they hatch, the first thing they see is not Mama but humans dressed in feathered costumes made of pillowcases (don't laugh). As they grow, the young birds learn to follow these humans, who carry around a small replica of an ultralight airplane and play the tape-recorded engine sounds. Eventually, the birds are ready for the real thing: they follow a real ultralight plane into the air. Time to head south for the winter!

This is no flight of fancy. The goal of Lishman's Operation Migration is to teach endangered birds new migration routes. If the old migration routes the birds have used for years are no longer safe for some reason, their ability to find new routes is the key to their survival.

Lishman's story would make a great movie. In fact, it did! The Hollywood movie was called *Fly Away Home*.

ROBOCOP VERSUS THE GRIZZLIES

Troy James Hurtubise has been run over by a three-ton pickup truck eighteen times. He has fallen, on purpose, off the edge of the fifty-metre-high Niagara Escarpment. His strongest friends have beaten him with two-by-fours and baseball bats and attacked him with a chainsaw.

Why? To test his "grizzly-proof" suit of armour!

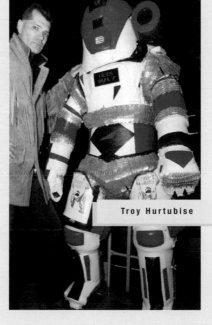

Troy Hurtubise

You see, Hurtubise wants biologists to learn more about grizzly bears. But close encounters with grizzlies can be life-threatening. So Hurtubise invented a bearproof suit. It's made of sixty-seven kilograms of titanium alloy, rubber, plastic, and chain mail. It is armed with a camera and a can of bear repellent. He got the idea for it from watching a sci-fi movie, *Robocop*. When he's wearing the suit, he looks like a futuristic sci-fi robot.

Hurtubise has yet to actually test the suit on a grizzly. On a test run in the Rockies, he stumbled in the incredibly stiff, heavy outfit and crashed to the ground. Oops! But ever hopeful, Hurtubise has a new bear-proof suit on the drawing board.

If you see a robot-like alien standing on the road, it's probably just Hurtubise waiting for a friend to drive by and run him over.

Let's see if this suit is black bear proof too. Go on, attack me! I'm ready!

Now, how can I get out of this tactfully?

GO-GETTERS

TERRY FOX launched his Marathon of Hope, a run across Canada to raise money and awareness for cancer research, in 1980. Starting in St. John's, Newfoundland, Fox, who'd lost his right leg to bone cancer a few years earlier, ran 5,373 kilometres to Thunder Bay, Ontario, before he was forced to quit because cancer was discovered in his lungs.

Inspired by Terry Fox, **STEVE FONYO**, who had also lost most of a leg to bone cancer, ran all the way across Canada (7,924 kilometres!) between March 1984 and May 1985. He too raised millions for cancer research.

Meanwhile, **RICK HANSEN** left Vancouver in March 1985 to travel, in a wheelchair, the equivalent of the distance around the world (40,073 kilometres). During his two-year Man in Motion tour, he wore out 117 wheelchair tires and 11 pairs of gloves. He also raised $20 million to help people with disabilities.

Steve Fonyo

Terry Fox

Rick Hansen

I'm Billy Bishop, the First World War flying ace from Owen Sound, Ontario. I take off at dawn and launch reckless, close-range attacks on enemy pilots. I'm a terrible pilot, but boy, am I a fantastic shot! Most fighter pilots last about ten days before they are shot down (and there are no parachutes!). I shot down seventy-two enemy planes—and lived to brag about it! I was awarded the Victoria Cross for a single-handed attack on a German airfield.

Billy Bishop

I'm the Great Farini (more boringly known as Bill Hunt). My hometown is Port Hope, Ontario, and that's where I crossed the Ganaraska River on a tightrope. My father was not impressed! Then, in 1860, I walked across a high wire over Niagara Falls.

I think I should do something biggest, best, first, or longest. Then I'd be famous too!
Well, you could be the first Canada goose to graduate from university with a degree in neurobiology.
That would take too long.
Okay then, how about becoming the first Canada goose to fly backwards from coast to coast?
I've got it! I'll be the first Canada goose to ride a moose up an escalator while playing a guitar! Let's go, Moose.

In 1982, **LAURIE SKRESLET** was the first Canadian to reach the summit of Mount Everest, the highest mountain in the world. Sharon Wood, the first Canadian woman to reach the summit, duplicated Skreslet's effort four years later.

PATRICK MORROW has had his ups and downs. He has climbed the highest mountain on each of the world's seven continents.

ARTHUR VILLENEUVE, a barber in the town of Chicoutimi, Quebec, decided to paint his house one day. He painted pictures inside, outside, on the ceiling, and everywhere else. He even painted the Saguenay River flowing down beside the staircase. (His wife forbade him to paint the refrigerator and stove.) Now his house is a big tourist attraction!

Incredible Inventions Ahead! You Saw Them Here First!

Why Would Anyone Invent That? Astounding Canadian Inventions

Canadians are full of great ideas ... and some not-so-great ones. The Canadians on this page don't see problems—they see solutions (and marketing opportunities!).

GO BACK TO SLEEP, ALEX!

Alexander Graham Bell was the kind of enthusiastic guy who would wake friends in the middle of the night to show them something he was inventing. His work teaching the deaf likely helped him develop the idea for the telephone. Each end of Bell's invention had a membrane like an eardrum. Sound waves would cause the membrane at one end to vibrate (the same way an eardrum vibrates when sound waves hit it). Electricity travelling through a wire would carry the pattern of this vibration to the other membrane. It would then vibrate in a similar pattern and make the original sounds. "Hello? Somebody answer the phone!"

Bell also invented (take a deep breath) kites that can carry people, one of the first gasoline-powered biplanes, a hydrofoil boat that set world speed records, a gizmo to get the salt out of seawater, ways to help teach deaf people, a breed of superior sheep, a phonograph, an iron lung for underwater divers, medical devices, electrical devices ... no end of useful and useless stuff!

Alexander Graham Bell

Invented in Canada by real Canada goose. Patent pending.

PABLUM

Did you eat pablum cereal as a baby? Bet you didn't know it was invented by three Canadian doctors in the late 1920s. They wanted a nutritious, vitamin-enriched, easy-to-prepare food for babies. Bet you just thought it was really yummy. Bet you dumped your pablum upside down on your head. (Ah, you were *so* cute!)

GREEN GARBAGE BAGS

In the 1950s, a man from Winnipeg, Harry Wasylyk, invented green garbage bags. His business was later bought by Union Carbide, which marketed the bags. They didn't really sell well until the late 1960s, however, and even then some customers didn't quite get the idea. They called the company to complain that the garbage collectors were taking away the bags with the garbage. They thought the bags would be emptied and then left behind so that they could be used again.

Don't forget that Canadian scientists invented the Canadarm!

Canada

Sure they run fast, but can they wag their tails?

BASKETBALL

Another slam dunk by a Canuck! Dr. James A. Naismith invented the game of basketball in 1891. At first, Naismith nailed peach baskets at either end of the gym and used them for the hoops. That's why the game was called *basket*ball. (Later, players got tired of climbing up to retrieve the balls from the baskets, so they cut out the bottoms to let the balls fall through!)

LACROSSE

First Nations tribes living around the St. Lawrence River invented lacrosse, but they called it baggataway. The ball they used was made of stuffed deerskin or strips of leather knotted together. There were sometimes hundreds of players on each team, and matches could go on for days. The game was used to help train warriors, so competition was fierce. Sometimes it resulted in severe injuries and deaths. The French called the game the *jeu de la crosse*, which is where the name lacrosse comes from.

ICE HOCKEY

One thing Canadians are good at is having a great time on ice and snow. So we invented ice hockey in the 1850s (some people say in Halifax, some say in Kingston). Students at McGill University in Montreal made up a set of official rules in 1875, and after that the game really caught on. In 1893, a hockey fan called Lord Stanley of Preston, Canada's governor general, forked over the money for a sterling silver bowl to use as a trophy. You guessed it—that trophy is now the NHL's Stanley Cup.

GINGER ALE

Shake it up! Canadian chemist and pharmacist John J. McLaughlin concocted the formula for Canada Dry Ginger Ale. He patented the recipe in 1907, and it's still a deep secret. His "champagne of ginger ales" is now sold worldwide.

Remember me, the Great Farini? When I'm not up to my acrobatic tricks, I'm an inventor. I invented folding theatre seats and parachutes. And I have a patent on the human cannonball act!

SNOWMOBILES

It figures that a Canadian would invent the snowmobile. Joseph-Armand Bombardier's first version, built in 1922, was simply a sled with a propeller on it. The heavy 1937 version was like a car sitting on skis and half-tracks. Then he found a lightweight motor, and the first Ski-Doos (he originally planned to call them Ski-Dogs, because he thought they would eventually replace dogsleds in the North) appeared in 1959.

LINES DOWN THE MIDDLE OF THE ROAD

I'll bet you dollars to doughnuts you've never asked yourself who came up with the brilliant idea of painting a line down the middle of the road to separate the lanes of traffic. A Canadian, of course! The first line was painted on a stretch of highway in Ontario in 1930. Canadians like to keep things safe, neat, and orderly on the road. No collisions, please. You stay on your side, and I'll stay on my side.

Big Things in Store

Big Roadside Attractions

Can you imagine the biggest Easter egg in the world? The largest lobster? Canadians from coast to coast to coast have built some gigantic things along the roadside, hoping to make a big impression on visiting tourists. Moose, cows, potatoes—check out these examples.

It might have difficulty getting airborne.

I'm statuesque!

Flintabbatey Flonatin's the name.

Gigantic **CANADA GEESE** are very popular subjects for statues. There's one outside of Lundar, Manitoba. Another is at Alf Hole Goose Sanctuary, near Rennie, Manitoba. Goose #3 is in Wawa, Ontario (wawa means "wild goose" in the Ojibwa language). That one is nine metres tall, made of steel, and weighs two tonnes.

Moose are also popular for statues. Mac is a seven-and-a-half-metre concrete moose in Moose Jaw (of course), Saskatchewan. **MAXIMILLIAN MOOSE** is six metres tall and lives in Dryden, Ontario. There's a third moose in Cow Bay (just outside of Dartmouth), Nova Scotia.

This is Josiah Flintabbatey Flonatin, nicknamed "**FLINTY**." He's quite a character. Actually, he really is a character—the hero of a science-fiction book that some gold prospectors found at this Manitoba spot in the early 1900s. When they later discovered gold here in 1914, they decided to name their mining claim Flin Flon, after the character in the book. (Get it? *Flin*tabbatey *Flon*atin.)

Are you sure he's the largest?
No, but I wouldn't argue with him.

Good to the last bite!

Meet **QUILLY WILLY** of Porcupine Flats, Saskatchewan. He claims he's the world's largest porcupine!

The **BIG NICKEL** is in Sudbury, which has the world's largest-known deposit of that mineral. (But guess what—this nine-metre-high nickel is actually made of stainless steel.)

The world's biggest **APPLE** is in Colborne, Ontario. Try sinking your teeth into this one! (Or buy the apple crumble pie instead.)

A red river cart? It's not red.
It's named after the Red River.
Is the Red River red?
In some places the clay is sort of reddish.

This giant pysanka, or painted **EASTER EGG**, is in Vegreville, Alberta, east of Edmonton. The egg is almost eight metres long, and it turns in the wind. Many families around Vegreville have ancestors who came to Canada from Ukraine long ago. They have a tradition of creating beautiful Easter eggs. Usually, the eggs are smaller than this one.

Yield right-of-way to the world's largest **RED RIVER CART**, in Selkirk, Manitoba. The carts were used for transportation on the Prairies during the 1800s. They could be hitched to an ox or a horse and could travel over rough or marshy ground. They even floated! Too bad they squeaked. Fortunately, this one isn't going anywhere.

Big oil job! This giant **OIL CAN**, six and a half metres high, is in Rocanville, Saskatchewan. It's dedicated to a resident who invented the squirting oil can.

It's an armoured tank? No, it's a monster **LOBSTER** in Shediac, New Brunswick—the lobster capital of the world!

Here's the world's largest **DUMP TRUCK**, in Sparwood, B.C.

Cool catfish sighted in Selkirk, Manitoba, the **CATFISH** capital of the world.

This isn't a complete list of big things, of course. There are many more, including:

- Smokey the Bear, outside Revelstoke, B.C.

- giant turtles in Turtleford, Saskatchewan (north of Saskatoon), and Boissevain, Manitoba (site of the annual turtle derby)

- an enormous tomahawk (over sixteen metres long) in Cut Knife, Saskatchewan

- an Indian head just outside of—can you guess?—Indian Head, Saskatchewan

- a giant muskie fish in Kenora, Ontario

- Jumbo the circus elephant in St. Thomas, Ontario (where the real Jumbo was hit and mortally wounded by a locomotive)

- a tomato-shaped tourist information booth in Leamington, Ontario, the tomato capital of Canada (where they make ketchup)

- Pinto McBean in Bow Island, Alberta, the bean capital of the West.

Keep reading—
it's not over yet.

WAY OUT

Is this the end of our great Canadian adventure?

I'm afraid so, Goose. But we'll always have the memories.

Hey, I remember that part—the asteroids smashing into earth!

Remember all those strange Canadian animals?

Present company excepted, of course.

I liked that fuzzy wuzzy Arctic woolly bear caterpillar, the one that froze every winter.

Remember all the explorers looking for the Northwest Passage?

Yeah, when they weren't getting lost, they were getting scurvy.

We saw some wild weather too, didn't we?

You're not kidding! Ice storms toppling transmission towers, chinooks gobbling up snow, tornadoes tearing about.

And quite the assortment of unusual people, places, and things.

Too darned many! My head is spinning.

So what do you think of Canada now that you've learned so much about it?

Too darned big! We should have explored Liechtenstein.

Say, Goose, I wonder ...

No more! Stop wondering! My head's full, and I can't fit any more in!

But Canada has so much more!

I know, but not today. I gotta go. I gotta ... um, fly south for the winter. Urgently!

Well, when you come back next spring, we'll go exploring again.

Sure, by then my head will be bigger.

Hard to believe it could get any bigger. Ha, ha.

Come and find me. I'll be in a Canadian bog.

With a frog? In the fog?

Now don't start that again.

You're gonna miss me, aren't you?

It will be a long winter, for sure.

Well, you live in Canada. What do you expect?

EXIT

Acknowledgements

This book is for all my wonderful young readers from coast to coast to coast (hey, that means YOU!)—those curious, clever, sometimes serious, but generally silly and sassy kids who appreciate the witty, warped, creative, and different spin that Dianne Eastman and I put on Canada in our books.

I would also like to acknowledge the British Columbia Arts Council for financial assistance during the writing of this book. Peter Jordan, Kim Poole, Peter Wood, Eric White, and Peter and Nancy Macek also helped in various ways with the research and writing of *Only in Canada!* — V.B.

Photo Credits

Care has been taken to trace ownership of copyright materials contained in this book. Information enabling the publisher to rectify any reference or credit line in future editions will be welcomed.

For reasons of space, the following abbreviations have been used:
CCRS: Canada Centre for Remote Sensing, Natural Resources Canada
CP: CP Picture Archive
GA: Glenbow Archives
HBCA: Hudson's Bay Company Archive, Provincial Archives of Manitoba
LPP: Lone Pine Photo
NAC: National Archives of Canada
NHML: Natural History Museum, London
PC: Parks Canada
VB: Vivien Bowers
VP: Valan Photos

Page 7 (Canada): courtesy CCRS; 9: VB; 13 (middle): Tom W. Parkin/VP; 14: courtesy CCRS; 15 (top to bottom): PC/B. Olsen/10.105.03.20(104), PC/B. Morin/06.60.08.07(08), VB; 16 (left, top and bottom) and 17 (lower left): courtesy CCRS; 17 (top): MEF/Publiphoto; 20: Herman H. Giethoorn/VP; 23 (top, left to right): Johnny Johnson/VP, Wayne Lankinen/VP, Royce Hopkins/LPP; 23 (middle): PC/W. Lynch/10.104.10.03(02); 24 (top, left): BC Archives/A-00347; 25: NHML; 26 (top): Gilbert van Ryckevorsel/VP; 26 (bottom): Francis Lépine/VP; 27: VB; 28 (centre): Aubrey Lang/VP; 29 (top, left): Wayne Lankinen/VP; 29 (centre): R.C. Simpson/VP; 29 (bottom, right): B. Lyon/VP; 30 (centre): John L. Bykerk/LPP; 30 (bottom, right): Barrett & Mackay; 31 (right): Clara Parsons/VP; 32 (left): PC/W. Lynch/01.11.03.05(102); 32 (top, centre): Stephen J. Krasemann/VP; 32 (bottom, centre): R. La Salle/VP; 33 (top to bottom): Dr. A. Farquhar/VP, John Fowler/VP, VB, Harold V. Green/VP, Wayne Lankinen/VP; 36 (left): NAC/C-000403; 36 (right): GA/NA-1677-10; 37: GA/NA-1807-11; 38 (left to right): NAC/C-003805, NAC/C-003806; 39 (top): NAC/A.P. Low/PA-051464; 39 (middle, left to right): NAC/C-003806, Richard Harrington/NAC/PA-129935; 39 (bottom, left): Richard Harrington/NAC/PA-129886; 40 (both): VB; 41 (upper): NAC/C-011050; 41 (lower): NAC/PA-031354; 42 (top to bottom): NAC/C-070165, NAC/C-034667; 43: NAC/C-073425; 44 (background): NAC/W. H. Cloverdale Collection of Canadiana/C-040372; 46: NAC/C-070250; 47 (clockwise, from top left): NAC/C-019550, NAC/C-006896, NAC/C-003131; 48: VB; 49 (left to right): NAC/C-147743, NAC/C-010089; 50 (from top to bottom): HBCA/1987/363-R-34/30 (N13504), HBCA/1987/363-R-34/33 (N11643)/J. Mills; 51 (left to right): NAC/PA-117943, NAC/C-001875, NAC/C-052177; 54 (left to right): NAC/C-001229, NAC/C-017338; 55 (centre, left): NAC/C-016877; 55 (centre, right): HBCA/1987/363-W-11415 (N7165); 55 (bottom, left): CCRS; 56 (middle): VB; 57: NAC/C-008373; 58: BC Archives/Frederick Dally/A-00350; 59: BC Archives/Bond/D-04549; 60: GA/NA-4938-32; 61 (left to right): GA/NA-990-6, GA/NA-1459-3; 63: CP/Andrew Vaughan; 65: Jiri Hermann/BHP Diamonds Inc.; 66 (left to right): CP/Dave Buston, VB; 67 (clockwise, from top left): CCRS, VB, CP/Bernard Brault, Sucaro Photography; 70: CP/Ari-Matti Rouska; 71: Johnny Johnson/VP; 72: CP/James Masters; 73: V. Wilkinson/VP; 74: PC/J. Woods/10.102.14.03(13); 75 (left to right): CP/Jacques Boissinot, CP/Ryan Remiorz, CP/Jacques Boissinot; 76–77: CP/Marianne Helm; 82 (top to bottom): GA/NA-862-2, NAC/PA-122479; 83: NAC/PA-164693; 84 (upper and lower): NAC/PA-016747, NAC/PA-051546; 85 (left to right): NAC/PA-117423, NAC/PA-122615, NAC/PA-133260; 86 (left to right): CP/Jacques Boissinot, CP/Peter Lennihan; 87 (clockwise, from top left): CP, CP/Chuck Stoody, CP/Tim Clark, NAC/PA-001654; 88 (left to right): NAC/C-014483, Robert Teteruek; 89 (top): courtesy of the Canadian Space Agency (www.space.gc.ca); 89 (left to right): Basketball Hall of Fame, Springfield, MA, NAC/PA-16239, Bombardier, Inc.; 90 (all) and 91 (left, top and middle): Henri Robideau; 91(left, bottom, and 3 on right): VB; 92 (top row, left): NAC/C-006896; 92 (second row, left to right): NAC/PA-133260, VB, VB, NAC/C-008373; 92 (third row, left to right): VB, NAC/001875, NAC/C-14483; 92 (fourth row, left to right): NAC/C-000403, NAC/PA-001654; 93 (from top to bottom, starting with second image): NAC/C-011050, Merman H. Giethoorn/VP, V. Wilkinson/VP, NAC/W. H. Cloverdale Collection of Canadiana/C-040372; Richard Harrington/NAC/PA-129935.

Index